Praise

Rick's approach to identifying and r
is a practical approach to discovering your true potential that
will have a powerful impact both personally and professionally.
Challenging against your own thought patterns and distorted
narratives, Rick has the ability to take clients on a journey of
self-discovery that changes everything and establishes patterns
for unlimited growth.

—Cristina Womack
President and CEO, Pasadena Chamber of Commerce

Rick is a friend, confidant, and mentor of mine. His easy way
of cutting through the clutter and focusing on ways to live,
interact, and bless those he comes in contact with is something
that I have directly benefited from. His shared knowledge in
Born Limitless is simple yet powerful and a message I know
will benefit you too.

—Chad Burke
President and CEO, Economic Alliance Houston Port Region

Anyone who has experienced Rick Torrison will testify that
there are few people in this world who can help you set a
vision for your life and unlock your human potential like
Rick can. The man is pure joy, compassion, energy, love, and
contribution bundled into one enthusiastic force. His desire to
see change in others is magnetic, and he stops at nothing to see
lives enriched. Having his words available to you in book form
is the type of 100-fold return you've been hoping for. Thank
you, Rick, for putting this together!

—Colt Charlebois
Founder of the ADAM Men's Movement

1

Through personal stories and practical experiences, Rick takes the reader on a journey of self-discovery and personal growth. When we can identify the limiting beliefs that hold us back and replace them with limitless beliefs, we move from a fixed mindset to a growth mindset.

—Dr. DeeAnn Powell
Superintendent of Schools, Pasadena ISD

Rick's insight and practical examples of limitless leadership have helped my team and me take our performance to the next level. By unlocking potential in others, Rick has a keen and unique ability to develop transformational leaders.

—Jeanna Bamburg
FACHE Chief Executive Officer
The Woman's Hospital of Texas, HCA Houston Healthcare

As someone who's dedicated a lifetime to unlocking human potential and leading courageously, I can't recommend Rick and his book Born Limitless highly enough. The path from constraint to endless possibility is beautifully navigated in these pages. Rick's simple yet potent strategies mirror the resilience and discipline I've advocated for, both on the battlefield and in personal growth. With riveting personal accounts and actionable wisdom, he shifts readers from a static perspective to a horizon of growth. Dive into this treasure if you're committed to truly unleashing your potential and shaping a boundless tomorrow.

—Marcus Truman
USAF Combat Rescue Officer (Ret)
Founder & Veteran Owner, Archangel Performance Coaching
Ph.D. Candidate in Psychology of Human Performance
M.A. in Leadership and Management, M.A. in Counseling
Certified Human Performance Specialist, Trainer, and Coach
"Live and Lead Courageously"

From limited to limitless, Rick helps you not only identify limiting beliefs and their source but also crush them and replace them with limitless ones. By unlearning things that may have helped you survive in the past but are no longer serving you, we break free from a fixed mindset to a growth mindset. Powerful!

—Tara Stone
SUCCESS & Empowerment Coach
#CommitivationNation
Thetarastone.com

By transparently sharing his real-world experiences, Rick instantly assures readers that they are not alone in their struggles. He then guides them toward moments of self-reflection and discovery, ultimately fostering a clear sense of purpose and igniting an internal passion to unleash their true potential!

—Everett L. Smith
Vice President of The Kaneka Foundation

Rick is a truly gifted and passionate coach and trainer. His experience, background, and expertise combine in just the right way to create massive impact in the lives of the people he touches. Through his words, you will experience a shift in your personal beliefs that will open the door to limitless possibilities for your future. If you are looking for a path forward in your life, let this be the first step on your journey.

—Eli Schaugh
Certified Master Success Coach
Master Practitioner of NLP
International Trainer of Effective Communication and Sales
CoachWithEli.com

Believing in ourselves that there are no limits to personal growth at all times can be discovered through the lens of Rick's personal stories and practical experience when we can identify the limiting beliefs that hold us back and replace them with limitless beliefs.

—Margie Pena
Community Developer of Community Initiatives, Baker Ripley

Rick's life experiences and storytelling allow you to find yourself in the story and see your way through to your personal transformation and growth. The power of crushing limiting beliefs that do not actually serve you and replacing them with new beliefs is the doorway to experiencing and walking in the limitless life we were created for.

—Yasmene McDaniel, MBA, MHA
Chief Executive Officer, HCA Houston Healthcare Southeast

I have known Rick for over 30 years and have seen how he has coached and helped countless people overcome limiting beliefs. We all have been designed with great potential, but we often need someone to help us unpack it. Rick is a master at this, not only with this book but as a coach and speaker.

—Todd Hopkins
Founder of Office Pride, Business coach,
International Best-selling author

BORN LIMITLESS

CRUSH LIMITING BELIEFS, CULTIVATE AN INFINITE MINDSET, AND UNLEASH YOUR TRUE POTENTIAL

OTHER BOOKS BY RICK TORRISON

Roadmap to Significance

BORN LIMITLESS

CRUSH LIMITING BELIEFS, CULTIVATE AN INFINITE MINDSET, AND UNLEASH YOUR TRUE POTENTIAL

RICK TORRISON

ethos
collective

Printed in the United States of America

Published by Ethos Collective™
PO Box 43, Powell, OH 43065
www.ethoscollective.vip

Identifiers:
LCCN: 2023915825
PaperbackISBN: 978-1-63680-202-2
Hardcover ISBN: 978-1-63680-203-9
eBook ISBN: 978-1-63680-204-6

Available in paperback, hardback, and e-book.

Any internet addresses (websites, blogs, etc.) and telephone numbers printed in this book are offered as a resource. They are not intended in any way to be or imply an endorsement by the author, nor does the author vouch for the content of these sites and numbers for the life of this book.

Some names and identifying details have been changed to protect the privacy of individuals.

To my mom—
Thank you for loving me without conditions
and believing in me even when I did not believe
in myself.

Table of Contents

Foreword

BY SAM SILVERSTEIN

The path one takes to reach their current state can reveal much about their character. As children, we lack control over this trajectory, with parents and other influential adults shaping our course. However, as adults, our choices wield a more direct influence over our destinations, our identities, and the impact we leave on the lives of those around us.

Rick Torrison was destined to pen this book. *Born Limitless* firmly asserts the belief that our circumstances do not determine our future and that greatness resides within each of us. While past experiences might leave us doubting our innate potential, embracing the belief that we can seize control of our future through the choices we make today is a powerful step towards uncovering and embodying our true potential.

My encounters with Rick Torrison have revealed an individual who consistently seeks and discovers the positive aspects and possibilities in life. Rick envisions the full potential of his coaching clients and the organizations he advises, effectively leading them to realize their capabilities.

Open yourself to the wisdom of Rick's profound words. Embrace Rick's mindset. Follow the path he lays out before you. The present moment is the ideal time to let Rick's experiences, accomplishments, and extraordinary vision for your future guide you in realizing your full potential.

Most individuals merely believe they comprehend their potential. The truly impactful figures in the world are those who refuse to be hindered by perceived limitations. They recognize that genuine potential extends beyond what meets the eye and comprehension. They understand that having a coach to direct, inspire, and motivate us will ultimately aid us in discovering what others have known all along—that we are Born Limitless.

—Sam Silverstein, CSP, CAPE

Founder, The Accountability Institute

*Author, No More Excuses, Non-Negotiable,
and The Accountability Advantage*

Past president, The National Speakers Association

Foreword

BY DOUG STRINGER

Throughout life's journey, we experience defining moments, people, times, and places that leave an indelible impression on us. I've met some amazingly gifted individuals and have forged some substantive and lasting friendships with people who inspire and motivate me. The most priceless commodities are not found in earthly treasures but in how we steward our time, friendships, and relationships.

What first struck me about Rick was his authentic pursuit of faith and, out of that faith, a genuine heart to empower and encourage those around him. We immediately became friends. There are people who come into our lives whose example provokes others to want to do better and dream greater. I've learned that some people simply happen to influence, while leaders determine to influence. Rick Torrison is such a person. The late Dr. Edwin Louis Cole, internationally recognized leader, author, and founder of a global organization, wrote in the foreword of one of my books, "Time like light makes things manifest. Given enough time, the real character of an individual will become known through their thoughts, words, and actions. Fame can come in a moment, but greatness comes with longevity."

Time has proven Rick to me personally on many levels. When we've partnered and endeavored to serve local communities, as well as facilitate national and international gatherings and initiatives together, I've seen firsthand his character and leadership exemplified.

Our true legacy does not come from the sermons we preach or how many follow us on social media. It's not the size of our organization or church. It is the lives we live before we enter the portals of eternity that will determine the influence we have and will leave for the next generation.

As I read through *Born Limitless*, I was reminded of a quote by D.L. Moody in the 1800's, "There are no limits to those who have been in the presence of the Lord." This book will help you to recognize that there are no limits to what is in store for you, in you, and through you.

Rick Torrison skillfully and experientially gives you tools for your life and leadership. It will not only inspire and motivate you, but it will enlarge your vision and dreams, and it will provoke you to accomplish more than you thought was possible. Regardless of any personal or corporate challenges you may have faced or are facing, you can step into a defining moment to leave a lasting imprint and impact for others to follow.

—Doug Stringer

Founder and President,
Somebody Cares America and Somebody Cares International

Author, Leadership Awakening,
Foundational Principles for Lasting Success

PREFACE

I WAS A MISTAKE

Born Limitless is ultimately about my belief that every one of us is born with potential and the ability to live a life of significance. That means *you*—regardless of the conditions of your birth or your current reality—were created for something greater.

Do you believe you were created for something *more*? Maybe you did at one time in your life, but you eventually gave up. If so, I don't blame you. Most people have remarkably low expectations for their lives. This is a big part of my personal story, and it's something I've seen countless times over the last twenty-five years I've spent coaching and counseling. This process is about creating an infinite mindset where you truly believe anything is possible.

I've worked with hundreds of people who once settled for a limited view (or "less-than" belief) about themselves and what was possible for their lives. I walked each one through my proven process to create new beliefs and walk them out of limiting beliefs to an infinite mindset. I shared that incredible process in my first book, *Roadmap to Significance*. But over the years, I've recognized that many of my coaching clients got hung up on the first step of the process: realizing their true potential. They had a limiting belief about themselves and what was truly possible. This is exactly where I had so much trouble before I discovered the limitless life.

So, I had to dive deeper—and that's what this book is all about.

If you want to change your life, crushing your limiting beliefs is essential. I define a "limiting belief" as a thought or state of mind we have owned as absolute truth, which then limits what we believe is possible. These limiting beliefs always hold us back in some way and prevent us from growing, achieving our goals, taking risks, and becoming the people we want to be. Many limiting beliefs come from the declarations and opinions of others, while others come from our environment or circumstances. We even have limiting beliefs that we have imposed upon ourselves. These beliefs, regardless of their source, become ceilings that keep us bound and settling for less than what is possible.

A *limitless* belief, on the other hand, challenges the status quo and draws us outside our comfort zone. It says, "You can do anything you set your mind to." A limitless belief is where possibilities begin and potential is realized. My belief, informed by my faith, is that every person is fearfully and wonderfully made from the time of their conception, and every single one was created for hope and a future—a limitless life.

Before you stop reading because you think I must have lived a charmed life with a wealth of opportunities, allow me to share a part of my story. Although today I am enjoying the fruit of a limitless life, the circumstances of my birth were anything but ideal.

I was born in Torrance, California, in 1965 (before you try to do the math, I'm fifty-eight at the writing of this book), the fourth child of an unwed mother. Her first two pregnancies ended in abortion, her third in adoption, and then there was me. With each pregnancy, she received an ultimatum from the birth father: "The child or me." It wasn't until she was pregnant with me that she decided she'd had enough of him.

She chose to keep me, and my father walked, leaving us homeless and thousands of miles from my mom's family in Illinois. Back in the sixties, it was taboo to be an unwed mother. My mom dreaded facing her family, so she tried everything to make it work in California. We moved from place to place for the first several months of my life until she finally found the courage to return home.

Mom did not receive a warm welcome. Her father was dying of cancer, and instead of telling him the truth about my birth, she lied. She told him she had gotten married but that my father had to remain in California. It wasn't until after my grandfather passed that Mom told my grandmother the truth.

It was a rough go for several years. My grandmother helped as she could while Mom worked several jobs to support us. The first nine years of my life were challenging, and my future was uncertain at best. The circumstances of my birth and early years created the backdrop for many of the limiting beliefs that shaped and impacted much of my later life. In the world's eyes, I never should have been born. I was a mistake.

But that wasn't the end of the story, as you'll soon see.

I can tell you from personal experience that a limitless life

> **A limitless life doesn't depend on the circumstances of our birth but rather on the choices of our lives.**

doesn't depend on the circumstances of our birth but rather on the choices of our lives. And the first step to living a limitless life is believing it's possible. Your current reality does not have to be your final reality. As I often tell members in my private Facebook community (The Limitless Leader), "Your past doesn't have to define your future."

The limitless life begins when you believe that you were created for *more*!

More isn't about stuff, titles, things, or possessions. It is about influence and impact, hope and a future. More is a legacy of a life well lived. More is a story of hope and redemption. It is the birthright of every human before and after life's unexpected detours. More is my story, and it can be your story. Circumstances of life, finances, and failed relationships do not define your more—*you* do.

I wrote *Born Limitless* from a lifetime of personal experiences, but don't think that I have arrived. Like all of you, I am a work in progress. I am . . . and I am becoming. That is why I'm excited for you to take this journey with me as I share the first and most important step in a process I have lived out and am still living. It's as simple as this—the repeated practice of believing and becoming all that we were created to do and be.

It's impossible to experience and sustain a limitless life without resetting the foundation of your beliefs. This book is about that process, focusing on your story and the obstacles and limiting beliefs that have shaped how you see yourself and that have established the actions and behaviors holding you back.

Being born limitless is our birthright, but it's also something we must contend for. It's not given to us—the process leading to the limitless life is filled with roadblocks and detours. The biggest challenge most of us face is that we don't believe that a limitless life is possible. Someone once said that if you can't conceive it, you can't achieve it. I prefer the motto of Napoleon Hill: "Whatever the mind can conceive and believe, the mind can achieve."

The process of discovering your limitless life begins with a vision and a new belief. You must believe something before you can be*live* it. This is the foundation of my proprietary coaching process. If you can't believe yet, please allow me to believe for you as we get started. I promise that by the time we are finished, you will not only believe it but will also be taking steps to be*live* it.

After you get a vision for your limitless life, I will ask you to honestly assess your current reality and use it as the baseline for your more. Your vision and your current reality are like bookends, and they will help you identify and crush the limiting beliefs and roadblocks that have kept you from discovering and releasing the more you were created for. Once your limiting beliefs have been replaced with limitless beliefs, you can begin to reframe and reset your future.

Your story is not over. How do I know? You're still breathing. Your story is like a book, filled with suspense, conflict, mystery, heroes, heroines, and villains. It does not matter how successful or challenging your story has been up to this moment—tomorrow's chapters have yet to be written. Everything that has happened up to this point in your life (the good, the bad, and the ugly) is only the foundation for everything that comes next! What matters now is the choice you make today and the story you choose to write tomorrow. Don't let your past (no matter how successful or challenged) define your future. Use your past to inform you and refine you but not define you.

If you want to discover freedom and unleash the power to "change your stars" (I love a good movie reference), then you will have to go through the difficult process of identifying and crushing the limiting beliefs that have been holding you back. You will be challenged. You may find yourself feeling offended, and you will come up with a thousand excuses for why you can't finish the book. But if you press through and give yourself some grace along the way, I can promise you will come out the other side emotionally stronger, mentally healthier, and ready to climb higher and reach further than ever before. You will believe that you were born limitless and begin walking out the more that is within you.

SECTION 1

BORN LIMITLESS

There is a short book published in 1903 by James Allen entitled *As a Man Thinketh*. It is one of my favorite books, and I read it at least once every year. Allen proposes the idea that what we think is what we will become: "A man is literally what he thinks, his character being the complete sum of all his thoughts."[2] Allen believes that in our "thought world," we hold the key to every condition that enters our life, and by working patiently and intelligently on our thoughts, we can remake our lives and transform our circumstances.

"Man is made or unmade by himself; in the armory of thought, he forges the weapons by which he destroys himself; he also fashions the tools with which he builds for himself heavenly mansions of joy and strength and peace."[3]

We all believe something. Is what you believe leading you to growth and life or decline and death?

1

Comfort Zone or Danger Zone?

All growth starts at the end of your comfort zone.
—Tony Robbins

H ave you ever taken a trip into the mountains? I remember the first time I drove along the eastern coast of the United States and experienced the wonder and beauty of the Blue Ridge Mountains. The Blue Ridge Parkway is an amazing stretch of highway that climbs over six thousand feet above sea level and meanders in and out and up into the mountains.

It was close to sunset when I came to the first scenic overlook. Thankfully, there were no cars behind me as I slammed on my brakes so I wouldn't miss the pull-off. I immediately saw why they called this range the "Blue Ridge." It looked like lakes filling the space between rolling hills that melted into the sunset. I was overwhelmed by a sense of calm and peace. I don't know how long I sat there, but I remember not wanting to leave.

I did move on, and the best part about that drive through the mountains was the excitement that came from knowing that every scenic overlook would be more spectacular than the last, each bringing an amazing view from a new perspective.

But what if I had come to that first scenic overlook on the Parkway and set up camp, never venturing any higher because I'd fallen in love with the beauty of that first spot? I might have stayed in the foothills forever when a few more miles up the road was another view even more breathtaking than the last.

Pause for a minute and think about where your life is currently "parked." You may be experiencing a scenic overlook—you've settled into your success and grown comfortable enjoying the view and the fruit of your labor. You've forgotten that just around the corner is something even greater, and if you don't challenge yourself to get up and keep moving, you will find yourself settling and missing out on the more that is waiting for you.

Or perhaps the "scenic overlook" feels more like a pit, and the only view is the challenges and the obstacles all around you. No matter how hard you try, you can't seem to get any traction, and you've eventually become tired and settled for something less than the best.

Wherever you find yourself, the truth is that you are not at the end of your story. If you are enjoying the good times and have gotten comfortable, there is another level waiting for you around the next bend. If you feel you are in the pit looking up, I want you to know that you are actually on a launch pad, preparing to be catapulted up and out.

Regardless of the situation you find yourself in, the challenge is not to settle in and become comfortable (yes, you can even become comfortable in the pit) where you're at. When that happens, you're in a comfort zone.

Comfort zones are places in our minds that represent the most common actions, reactions, and interactions in our lives. A comfort zone is like a boundary or fence line that we set up that gives us a sense of safety and security. Fences do more than keep things out—they lock us in. Comfort zones are great places to visit, but I am not sure we want to live there.

I'll tell another mountain story to illustrate my point. I was blessed to travel to Cape Town, South Africa. While I was there, I visited Tabletop Mountain. It was an incredible tram ride to the top. The view went on for miles, and I could see Cape Town below and the Indian and Atlantic Oceans at the same time. The view was breathtaking, and I could smell a mixture of the city and the ocean in every breath. The top of the mountain has its own ecosystem—the weather was significantly cooler, and it seemed I was walking in the clouds.

Back down in the city, as I was visiting and getting to know some of the locals, I shared with them the moving and powerful experience I'd had on the mountain. I'll never forget their response. They casually said, "Oh yes, it is a pretty mountain. I drive by it every day, but I've never actually been to the top. We locals don't think about it very often." They had become so comfortable with the beauty of their familiar surroundings that what was spectacular to visitors had become common to them. I remember thinking, *I hope my perspective on the world is never reduced to seeing the beauty and the greatness all around me as something normal.*

This is what it's like when we allow ourselves to camp out in our comfort zones. You may have traveled long and worked hard to get where you are. You may be tired from the journey and want to stop, rest, and catch your breath. Before you know it, you have set up camp and settled in. The danger comes when we believe that our current experience, this "scenic overlook," is the best it can get, or this is all there is. After a while, we become blind to our surroundings. We either lose the awe of the view or settle for the pit we have called home. What was once a comfort zone has become a danger zone.

If you are currently in a comfort zone, it's OK. I understand—I have been there, and I will probably visit a comfort zone again. The problem is not *visiting* a comfort zone, the problem comes when we set up shop and replace the comma in our life with a period. When we settle into a comfort zone, we stop growing, and that's when the comfort zone becomes a danger zone.

I once heard it said that if we are not growing, we are dying. I am not sure if that is biologically true, but it does cause me to stop and examine my life and what I am doing to challenge my comfort zones and places of growth. This book is about believing we are not at the end of our story—there is more growth, opportunity, impact, and influence we can have on the people and world around us. The challenge I have found with growth is that it never happens when we are in our comfort zone. Successful author, coach, and speaker Tony Robbins put it this way in his book *Unlimited Power*: "If you feel really comfortable, chances are you've stopped growing."

As we begin this journey toward our infinite mindset and limitless living, may I challenge your current mindset—those beliefs that you hold about yourself, your life, and your future? It has been my experience in twenty-plus years of coaching that we all have a set of beliefs that we live from and influence the things we say and do. These beliefs, true and false, impact every area of our lives. They become a filter through which we view everything.

I promise I will not ask you to think anything or do anything that I have not thought or done myself. The process is simple, but it won't be easy. Whenever we challenge our mindset, we run the risk of discovering things we do not like. We may discover that these things we have been holding on to for much of our lives have become very comfortable and familiar. If I am honest, there are times I really like comfort and familiarity. They are safe places, but they very rarely lead to growth and never to discovering the greatness that is within you.

Your mindset will either propel you through discomfort and moments of discouragement—driving you forward toward your more and a limitless life—or it will confine you in the tomb of your past, keeping you from discovering and walking out the more you were created for.

How can you know if your comfort zone has become a danger zone? You no longer see your current situation as a place you're passing through but rather as a place where you've settled in (for better or worse). You have been there so long that it has become normal—a way of life.

- You had a dream when you were younger, and then "life" happened. You forgot about the dream or have dismissed it as the idealism of youth.

- You were on a career path with CEO as the goal; you were working hard, progressing through the promotions, and then the company sold, or the leadership decided to go in a different direction, and you let go of that goal and settled into the comfort of middle management.

- You had the vision to start your own company, planning to work at your current job for a few more years and then take the money you were investing and launch a business. Then life happened, you lost your job, and your investments dried up.

- There was a special someone you couldn't wait to marry and start a new life with, but they decided they no longer felt the same way, and you are back to being alone.

Failures and disappointments can lead to overwhelm and cause us to settle in, stop taking risks, and set up camp in the safety of our comfort zones. If this is where you find yourself, keep reading. Your story is not over yet. On the other hand, don't allow success and progress to keep you from recognizing the areas of your life where you have allowed yourself to become comfortable.

Take a few minutes before moving on and identify the areas in your life where you may have begun to settle in. If you keep moving from this place, do you believe there is a greater "view" up ahead? If the answer is yes, then take a moment to honor and celebrate where you are and the work it took to get there, and then stand up, pack your things, brush the dust off, and start walking.

It is time to get out of your comfort zone. This place you are living in, the one you have called "normal," is about to be shaken up and turned upside down. It may seem awkward and uncomfortable at first, but I promise it will be worth it.

Sometimes, the hardest step is the first one. That first step is to name your comfort zones and the beliefs associated with them. Identify those places you have accepted as normal, bring them out of the shadows and into the light, and dare to dream again. One of the most powerful questions I use in my coaching is, "How does having that belief serve you?" This question confronts the fruit or lack of fruit that holding that belief has in our lives.

Here is another truth in case this assignment feels overwhelming: you don't have to figure it all out right now. Your shift—the first step into that limitless life and the more you were created for—begins with a mustard seed of belief. If you are not familiar with mustard seeds, I encourage you to search the internet for a picture of a mustard seed and then search for images of the mustard tree. It is amazing what can come from something that seems so insignificant. Trust that the light you see off in the distance, the one beginning to pierce the darkness of the tunnel you're in, is a ray of hope, possibility, and the restoration of the belief that you were created for more than the reality you currently find yourself in. Believe!

2

I Believe—Help My Unbelief

All things are possible for one who believes.
—Mark 9:23b (ESV)

The first step to moving out of your comfort zone to your growth zone is to acknowledge where you are right now—then you must believe there is more. This may be difficult if you have been in this comfort zone for so long that it feels normal. The challenge is to shift your belief and the mindset that says, "Where I am is good enough." As we begin, you do not need to know what the more is or even how to get there. You simply start with a mustard seed of faith that says, "I believe there is more."

The title of this chapter actually comes from a Bible verse. Whether or not you're a person of faith, this is a great example of where we often find ourselves. In the story, Jesus encounters a man whose child is suffering from a great illness. The father asks Jesus for his help: "If you can do anything, have compassion on us and help us."

Jesus responds: "'If you can'! All things are possible for one who believes."

Immediately, the father cries out, "I believe; help my unbelief!"

This is where I often find myself. I am not without belief, but my beliefs are limited. There's a ceiling on what I think is possible that's causing me to settle. The beginning of the breakthrough to the limitless life we were born and created for often starts with the declaration, "I believe—help my unbelief." This statement sets the foundation and creates the opportunity for something more, something greater than where we currently find ourselves. Beliefs are the key that will unlock the door to our limitless life.

We all have beliefs, but as I have already mentioned, not all of our beliefs are serving us and leading us toward growth. What we must understand about beliefs is that they drive our behaviors. The challenge is that most of us don't truly know what we believe or why we believe what we do. Our beliefs are in our subconscious and are born out of experiences and influences that accumulate throughout our lives. We aren't born with a set of beliefs—a newborn is a blank slate. The environment we are raised in, the experiences we go through, and the people who surround us write on that blank slate and begin to influence the beliefs that we develop about ourselves. They influence what we believe about who we are, who we can be, and what is possible. They also define how we see the world and how we choose to engage in relationships.

Forgive my language, but this can be the crappy part of our lives. As babies, young children, and even teenagers, we often don't have any say in the experiences and influences that have such a significant impact on our beliefs. Even in the most positive of environments and with a loving and caring family surrounding us, our young lives may be marked in detrimental ways. An adult's innocent comment, betrayal by an authority figure, undeserved punishment . . . these things cause us to define ourselves in ways that are "less-than."

Our limiting beliefs are typically easiest to identify by examining our feelings rather than our conscious thoughts. It is important as we get started to acknowledge that our feelings are significant and real, but they are not always based on truth. It is often in the interpretation of our feelings that our beliefs are formed.

Although I was raised without a father in the home, there was never a moment when I did not feel loved or valued by my mother, my grandmother, and my uncle, all of whom took turns raising me. But I knew I was different. My home and family didn't look like those of my friends, and I felt it everywhere I went. This feeling began to influence what I thought and believed about myself despite the love I was shown. One of the first examples I can remember is how I felt different playing Little League baseball—everyone seemed to have a dad helping at practice except me. I felt it at a friend's home, seeing two parents lovingly engaging their kids and sitting around a table together for dinner. I felt it when people asked me where my father was.

There were many comments, looks, and subtle reactions from others that I didn't recognize at the time, but that had a great impact on what I believed about myself, my family, and my future. This is where my limiting beliefs about myself began. I felt inadequate and like I didn't belong, and therefore, I had to work twice as hard to fit in. I know, looking back, that my circumstances were not my fault, and I had no control over them, yet they significantly shaped my view of myself and my relationships—how I grew up, interacted with others, and lived my life.

One experience, in particular, filled me with shame and fear and forever changed the way I related to others. My best friend in fourth grade was a boy we'll call Matt. He lived two doors down in the "Kool-Aid house." You know, the kind of place all the kids wanted to go after they got done playing to get a glass of Kool-Aid and a crunchy peanut butter sandwich. Matt had a great family—two parents, a brother, and two sisters. Matt's oldest sister was Susan, and she would babysit me when my mom wasn't able to make it home from work at a decent hour.

I was in fourth grade when Susan initiated a physical encounter with me. In that moment, my innocence was stolen. I was too young to understand the experience, but I knew it was wrong. I felt shame and a sense that I must have done something to invite the encounter. I stopped going over to Matt's house, but the shame and guilt kept me from saying anything to my mom or anyone else.

That experience eventually shaped how I viewed myself and the women in my life. The trauma and its effects lasted well into my adulthood, impacting every relationship and, eventually, my marriage. I lived with the belief that I was not good enough for a healthy relationship for so long that I thought it was normal. The shame, fear, and self-loathing from this belief shaped my behaviors until it almost cost me my marriage. Thankfully, my freedom came when I was led through a process similar to what I am sharing in this book. I exposed my wrong beliefs, identified the source, and began the hard but necessary work of replacing lies with truth.

Why do I share this with you? Because we all have stories that marked us and impacted how we view ourselves and others. In a way, we all have lenses through which we view life. The different events of our lives can mark up the lenses through which we view our current reality, our future possibilities, and ourselves. The more negative experiences we have, the blurrier our lenses become.

Have you ever been to an optometrist? I was forty years old when I had my vision examined for the first time, and I remember it well. The doctor put the machine in front of my eyes and clicked through different lenses, asking me simple questions like "Is it better like this?" After he had manipulated the lenses for the last time, it was as though I had been blind, and now I could see. I had no idea how poor my vision had become until I tried looking through new lenses.

My childhood experiences distorted the lenses through which I would see the world for years to come. More importantly, these experiences impacted how I viewed myself. Thankfully, I found help, hope, and healing. I was able to clean my lenses, and when I did, the view of my life, my marriage, and my future opened. The possibility that there might be more to life than what I was experiencing seemed real for the first time.

Even then, discovering the possibility of *more* did not mean that I started walking in it. The limiting beliefs I'd formed in childhood were deep and took some time to identify and conquer. I want you to hear me as you start this journey: freedom comes in phases. Don't try to jump the Grand Canyon in one leap. If you build a bridge and start walking, I promise you will get to the other side.

> **Discovering the possibility of *more* did not mean that I started walking in it.**

Sometimes, the hardest part is getting started. That first step is often the most difficult. The truth is we don't know what we don't know, and so we often don't know where to begin or how to take that first step. The first step can often be found in the questions we are willing to ask and answer.

Here are my questions for you:

- What is your story? What is the source of the beliefs that are not serving you?
- How has your story affected the lenses through which you view life? Relationships? Yourself? Your future?
- What are the limiting beliefs you have formed and owned for so long that you have called them normal?
- Where have these beliefs shown up, and how have these beliefs put a ceiling on your growth and success?

I hope you can hear me when I tell you that the limitless life you were born for is waiting for you. It begins with simple belief. The life you are living, no matter how successful or challenged, is not as good as it gets. The problem is that your past has affected your lenses and caused you to believe a lie. Once you believe a lie, you begin to be*live* that lie. Your behaviors start to match your beliefs, and you end up with this imaginary ceiling over your life. Don't you think it is time to break through that ceiling?

If you are going to change how you are be*living*, you will first have to change what you are believing. One of the first belief changes is that your limitless life is not defined by your circumstances and experiences. The truth that you were born limitless is not validated by anything you do or don't do—it is simply true! Once you choose to believe it, you can begin the journey to be*live* it.

So here is your action for this chapter. It is simple. If you are ready to move on, you need to make this declaration over your life:

I believe I was born limitless!
I believe I was created for more!

This is the foundation for everything that comes next. If you are up for the challenge, I want you to write these declarations down on a sticky note—actually, several sticky notes. Place those sticky notes on your bathroom mirror, your computer monitor, your refrigerator, and anywhere else you visit often. Declare these statements out loud daily. You are committed to what you confess. Your limiting beliefs did not get to where they are overnight; the journey to your freedom will take time. Your first step in jumping the Grand Canyon of limiting beliefs is to declare it is possible.

The next chapter is foundational to the process. It is important to understand that you will stumble and fail along the way, but that does not make you a failure. The first limiting belief we must all address is this idea that "it is too late for me—I have failed so many times that it doesn't matter anymore." This is a lie we all believe, and it is time to replace it with the truth.

I believe in you! But more important is the belief you have in yourself. Remember, you don't have to have it all figured out right now, you simply need to recognize the starting place and believe. "I believe; help my unbelief."

3

Failing Doesn't Make
You a Failure

There will be failures and mistakes and criticism. If we want to be able to move through the difficult disappointments, the hurt feelings, and the heartbreaks that are inevitable in a fully lived life, we can't equate defeat with being unworthy of love, belonging, and joy. If we do, we'll never show up and try again.
—Brené Brown, *Daring Greatly*

I love the quotation above. No one ever promised that life would be easy, simple, and free from trials and tribulations. Life, as we know all too well, is filled with both joys and sorrows, successes and failures. Brené Brown says that we cannot associate the defeat and challenges of our lives with our self-worth. Once we do, we have chosen to adopt a life that is less than what we were created for. Success or failure comes from what we believe about ourselves in the midst of the good, the bad, and the ugly experiences of life.

Have you ever felt that your life is filled with bad breaks and missed opportunities? No matter how hard you try, you can't seem to get ahead. At some point, the struggle wore you down, and you decided that this was as good as it was going to get. You may never say that out loud, but you have begun to believe it, and we live what we believe.

If you've found yourself on the side of failure, join the club. The danger comes when we allow our shortcomings to shape our beliefs about ourselves and our futures. As you go through the process I've laid out in this book, you will need to face your mistakes and poor choices. I will have you call out places where you have failed, but it is important that you don't get stuck there. John C. Maxwell, one of my mentors, told me that in order to go up or go higher in your life, you will have to go through. To go through it, you must shift your belief about the mistakes and failures you have experienced. Just because you failed doesn't mean you are a failure. I love what Joyce Meyer says about failure: "No matter how often I fail, I am not a failure unless I quit trying." [4]

Why do we believe that the most successful people never make mistakes? In fact, the opposite is true: the most successful people are the ones who fail the most and keep getting up. They are the ones who did not allow their mistakes to define them and refused to see themselves as victims.

If everyone who failed was a failure, we wouldn't have the light bulb, the telephone would not exist, no one would know Michael Jordan's name, Abraham Lincoln would never have become president, space travel would only exist in science fiction novels, and I wouldn't be writing this book. I cannot think of one thing that has made any significant impact on our world that was successful the first time. Zig Ziglar said, "Remember that failure is an event, not a person."

Not convinced yet? Here are some more fails-not-failures that you may not have known about:

- **15 times**—Richard Branson launched companies before Virgin Galactic.
- **25 times**—Tim Ferris's book The 4-Hour Work Week was rejected by publishers.
- **1,009 times**—Colonel Sanders, founder of KFC, was turned down when he tried selling his fried chicken recipe.
- **1,500 times**—Sylvester Stallone was rejected when he tried selling his script and himself in the film Rocky.
- **5,126 times**—James Dyson created failed prototypes of his vacuum cleaner.
- **10,000 times**—Thomas Edison created failed prototypes of his electric bulb. [5]

It's fair to say that not one of you reading this book knew how many times Colonel Sanders was turned down or how many times Sylvester Stallone was rejected. What we do know is whether we like the original recipe or extra crispy (I'm an extra-crispy guy myself), and if I asked for your favorite *Rocky* movie, you could quickly name it. No one thinks about how many times Edison failed when they turn on the light switch in their home. So, the real question I want to ask you is not "Have you failed?" but "How many times are you willing to get back up when you do?"

> The failures you've experienced along the way are only stepping stones to your future, not stumbling blocks.

To move forward in the pursuit of the limitless life you were born and created for, you will have to believe that the failures you've experienced along the way are only stepping stones to your future, not stumbling blocks—the difference is all in the way you approach them.

Our beliefs have a direct impact on our behavior. When we believe we are a failure and engage in negative self-talk or receive negative talk from others, we will begin to act out those beliefs.

Here are a few thoughts for you to consider as you move forward in this book. Allow these statements to shift your thinking about the mistakes and failures you have experienced. Return to these statements as you read.

- Failing is not personal. It does not define you or determine your value and worth. It simply reminds you that you are human.
- The quickest way through a moment of failure is to take immediate and full responsibility for the part that you played. Own it, don't run from it, be courageous, and accept responsibility. This will quickly shift the conversation away from your actions to your character.
- Choose to grow and learn from every failed action. Learn from the mistake and make the necessary adjustments moving forward.

Declare the following over yourself:

**I am not defined by how many times I fail
but by how many times I get back up.**

This is the first and most important belief that you must have to discover and experience the limitless life. It's from this foundation that we will identify and crush the rest of your limiting beliefs. Your best is yet to come; you are a person of purpose, value, and destiny. It is time for you to discover the miracle that you are.

4

The Miracle of You

For you created my inmost being; you knit me together in my mother's womb. I praise you because I am fearfully and wonderfully made; your works are wonderful, I know that full well.
—Psalm 139:13–14

I f you're reading a book about crushing your limiting beliefs and unleashing your true potential, you may be pursuing that most elusive question—What is my purpose? In my coaching practice, I help people work on identifying and clarifying their purpose more than anything else. In fact, it was my search for purpose that led me to discover the limitless life.

We often associate purpose with our careers, ministries, and passions. What I've found over the years is that our purpose is not as much about reaching a destination as it is about our value. Before we can discover and walk in our purpose, we must first believe that our life is worth something. If we do not believe we have value, we will not pursue our purpose. What's the point in pursuing purpose when we do not believe that we have anything to offer the world around us?

When I talk about value, I need to share some of my deepest beliefs. These are rooted in my Christian faith. I did not grow up with this faith, and I wasn't looking for it, but it found me and changed everything. I am not expecting you to believe as I believe—

If we do not believe we have value, we will not pursue our purpose.

you don't even have to be a Christian to experience the transforming power of the principles and practices I am sharing with you in this book. But my faith in Jesus is inseparable from my belief in the purpose and worth of every human being.

I absolutely believe that your life is a miracle. You are uniquely created; there is no other person in the world exactly like you. It's like fingerprints and snowflakes—no two are exactly alike.

How do I know that you are worth something? Because I believe God created every human being on purpose and for a purpose. In other words, there are no accidents or mistakes. No circumstance, condition, person, or quality of life has the right to determine your value, worth, and purpose—the limitless life that you were born and created for is a birthright, and it begins when you believe it.

Perhaps you don't think you struggle with knowing your value. You had an amazing childhood, a great family, and lots of opportunities. But let me ask you this: Do you have any unrealized dreams or unfulfilled goals? Are there issues in your life that keep coming up, and you can't seem to get any traction or make sustained progress? Although successful in most areas, do you find yourself frustrated and giving up in other areas, making the excuse that you're "just not good at (fill in the blank)" or that it must not be "something you are supposed to do"? You've given up because you can't seem to break through, even though you feel strongly this is something you are to pursue.

It is possible to be successful and confident in one aspect of life while feeling utterly incapable and a failure in others. We all have areas where we do not value ourselves very highly, so we ignore them or pretend they are not important. If I've learned anything through all of my coaching and counseling, it is that we are holistic people—the challenges in our lives that we fail to address tend to limit our overall success.

What if your life's purpose and the impact and influence you believe you can have on others is not found in what you do but rather in how you value your life? You have a purpose, something you are called to do, but you will struggle to find it if you do not see your own worth. Discovering your value will help you discover your individual purpose.

I believe in a universal purpose we all share that is tied to positively impacting and influencing the people and world around us. Every one of us is born with the potential to make a positive impact. Unfortunately, many of us—myself included—have allowed the circumstances of our birth and life, the disparaging declarations of those around us, and a perceived lack of opportunity to shape our thinking about our true worth and value.

Let me be clear about the starting place for being born limitless: you have value and worth because you were created with a purpose in mind. If there is no Creator, then you are simply an accident shaped by experience and circumstance. Even if this is what you believe, you do not have to remain as you are. We all have the ability to change what we think and what we believe. We have the power to choose different behaviors and responses to the life we find ourselves in. Our limitless life is still found in our beliefs.

Your life holds within it value and limitless potential. No matter what it looks like right now, you have the final say about your future! I understand you may not feel like it, but that doesn't make it any less true. I also understand there are gaps between making a declaration and believing it, acting on that belief, and experiencing the fruit of it in our lives. This book is about bridging those gaps.

To paint a picture of this, let me share another personal story with you. Both of my children were adopted from birth, three years apart. My wife, Melinda, and I were present when they were born and got to bring them home with us from the hospital. I do not have time or space here to share the full miracle of their adoption stories, but God knew what he was doing when he connected us with their birth mothers and decided that they were to be brother and sister.

My son and daughter have similar stories, but their mothers were incredibly unique. When they got pregnant, my son's birth mother was sixteen years old, and my daughter's birth mother was seventeen. The conception of both of my children was anything but planned or desired. These young girls became pregnant as a result of violent actions they had no control over and did not ask for. Instead of pursuing an abortion as the world was telling them to, they determined to give birth to these children and find a good home and family to raise them.

This is where their stories begin to differ. My son's birth mother came from an intact and supportive family, and the option to keep the child and raise him was something they seriously considered. My daughter's birth mother had a different background—a challenging childhood and years in the foster care system. She had little to no family support and was strongly encouraged to abort her child. She happened to be under the foster care of our family friends, and they encouraged her to consider adoption by sharing our son's story.

Both of these young women are strong and courageous; they are my heroes. I have a special admiration for my daughter's birth mother—she had everything working against her, and the world would have justified her if she had chosen to abort her daughter. Thankfully, both women chose life, and we have had the pleasure, privilege, and honor of raising their babies to become a powerful and purposeful young man and young woman.

Why do I share this? Because of the circumstances of my children's conception, our culture would define the pregnancies as unwanted and declare the babies disposable. Some people were labeled before they were even born. These labels often contribute to underlying beliefs that do not simply go away because someone grows up in a loving, stable home. I have had the honor and pleasure to work with many adoptive families, and I've also processed with my own children the underlying feeling of abandonment, which can lead to a devaluing of self and a loss of identity. Adopted children often grow into adults who have unconsciously placed a ceiling on what they are capable of or what they deserve. This occurs because they believe their value is tied to the circumstances of their conception or conditions surrounding their birth.

Reading the stories above, you could easily conclude that these children were never meant to be born into this world. That was how my children saw themselves, even though they were being raised in a loving, supportive, and stable home. This is also how I saw myself for most of my life. I believed that I was a mistake, not good enough, and not worthy of hope and a future. I deduced from my circumstances that I was unworthy of love, belonging, and joy. I lacked real value.

What changed for me? I went through a crisis of belief. I knew I needed a new narrative, but I didn't know where to find it or even how to begin. Then, I came to the point where I realized that no matter how hard I tried, I could never break through on my own. I needed help. The breakthrough for me began when I met my future wife. Melinda was a woman of faith from a family of faith, and she introduced me to a relationship with Jesus. For the first time, I began to see myself as a person of value. I realized that I wasn't an accident or a mistake and that my value was not determined by the circumstances of my conception or the conditions of my birth. My value and the limitless life we are talking about already existed within me because God created me.

I wish I could tell you the transformation happened quickly, but it did not. Even though I was told I had value and worth, it took years for me to really believe it and change the narrative. I didn't have the right influences around me calling me higher, challenging my limiting beliefs, and showing me a way to replace them with the truth. That is largely why I am writing this book. If one person can be encouraged by my message and see their true value and a map to their freedom, then all the work was worth it.

Let me ask you to consider your own story. What determines your value? While you may feel confident in some areas, what are those areas that you minimize or pretend don't exist? Where are the ceilings in your life?

Here's the truth: the greatness inside of you—the limitless life—is not something you can earn or achieve. It is not something you can buy, and no one can give it to you. Your incredible value and the fact that you were born limitless is true regardless of what you think about it and what experience tells you about it. This is your birthright! The journey of Born Limitless begins with you receiving and believing this to be true. From this place of belief, you can begin to change your behaviors and experience different outcomes—that is what this book is going to help you do.

As we bring this chapter to a close and turn a corner in the book, I want to set a foundation to build on. Hold on—I am about to dump a whole lot of "I believes" on you.

I believe, with all that I am, that you were born on purpose for a purpose, but you will never realize that purpose until you own your great value and a limitless life as your birthright.

I believe that God created you in love with hope and a future in mind.

I believe that there are no accidents or mistakes when it comes to your life, your conception, and your birth.

I believe that the circumstances of your life—the good, bad, and ugly experiences—do not define you or your future but rather inform you and refine you.

I believe that your limitless life is locked up and waiting to be released.

I believe that you were created for more—not more stuff, but more influence and impact. No matter how challenging or successful your life has been, your current reality is not the end of your story. In fact, it is simply the launchpad to your future.

I believe in you and the limitless life you were born and created for.

So here's my challenge as we turn the page. You do not have to fully believe what I just shared with you, but I would ask you to consider it and declare it over yourself, your life, and your future. Remember—your beliefs are like lenses that have been smudged and cracked over the course of your life by your circumstances and experiences. You've looked through them for so long that you can't imagine seeing yourself or the world a different way. These beliefs have become your normal.

Your lenses have impacted how you live and the outcomes that you have experienced in your life. If you are not satisfied with those outcomes and are ready to break through and experience this limitless life that you were born for, then it's time to clean up your lenses. It's time to create a new narrative, and that new narrative begins with a belief and a declaration. The transformation will come, but not without a fight. Like a caterpillar before metamorphosis, we must discern the times of our transformation and decide to go through the struggle. It is in the struggle that we become stronger and put to death our old self so that the new may be born. The difficulty is a sign that we are alive.

If you are ready, before you turn the page, will you make the following declarations out loud?

I am created for more—more influence and impact, more future and more hope.

I believe that I have great value and was born limitless. This is my birthright, and I choose to walk in it.

I challenge you to say these declarations out loud daily while looking at yourself in the mirror for the next thirty days. This anchors the thoughts into your subconscious, which is the place where true change and transformation happen.

Remember, it does not matter how challenged or successful you are—there is something more, something greater for you. You were born limitless. Let the journey to releasing that limitless life begin.

SECTION 2

YOU ARE HERE

Every GPS needs two locations to work properly. If you fail to input either one, you will never reach your destination. One location is obvious—the destination you desire to reach. The key to the destination is that it must be clear and exact. If you desire to eat at Hugo's (our favorite Mexican restaurant in Houston), you do not set "Mexican restaurant" as the destination in your GPS. Do you know how many Mexican restaurants there are in Houston? Neither do I, but I know it's a lot!

Setting a clear destination or vision, whether short-term or long-term, is where I begin with every coaching client. It is a critical factor in why many of us have never reached our personal or professional dreams—we failed to clearly define where we desired to go. That's why I wrote The Roadmap to Significance—to help people input their destination into their life's "GPS."

But for hundreds of my clients, clarifying their destination turned out to be the easy part. The challenge came when we attempted to honestly assess their current reality.

That's the second vital location for the GPS: the starting location. Think about it—what happens if you don't have your current location set correctly in the GPS? It won't matter how clear your destination is. If your starting point isn't right, you'll never arrive. Figuring out where you are involves examining what you believe. If you do not understand the beliefs that are impacting where you are and where you want to go, you will never arrive safely. You may make progress, but the limiting beliefs will always lead you back to where you started.

This next section is all about getting a clear picture of your current reality. Without that, everything else you do will eventually fall away, and you will find yourself back where you started. We will discuss the experiences that shape us, the beliefs that drive us, and the behaviors that have defined us up to this point. When you understand where you have come from, you are better able to decide where you are going.

If you take it seriously, this process will not be easy. This will be the only time that I invite you to look back at the journey of your life and identify those markers that have shaped you and affected the lenses through which you are viewing your current reality and your future. You will have to look in the mirror and ask yourself some difficult questions: "How did I get here? Where exactly am I?"

There is one last thing you must do before you continue. You must decide that where you are is not where you want to stay. You must choose to step forward even if the path is not clear and the destination is still to be determined. For some, this is a simple step, and they have already started walking. For others, it is a scary proposition. But for all of us, the key is that we must take the next step. Don't worry about the size of the step—take the next step. Or as the great philosopher Dory reminds us, "Just keep swimming . . . just keep swimming!" [6]

5

Don't Forget to Flush!

If you really want to do something, you'll find a way.
If you don't, you'll find an excuse.
—Jim Rohn

You are about to enter the "no but" zone. You may want to get another sticky note and write "NO BUTS ALLOWED" and post it on your computer screen or mirror. By making this statement, you have now brought into your consciousness the word but. I hope that you will notice every time you use this word.

It's a phenomenon called "frequency bias." Let's say you are thinking about buying a new car. You've identified the make and model you want, you've researched it online, and you may have even gone to a dealership to check it out. All of a sudden, it seems that everyone owns that car. You begin to see it all over the place, but it's not like all your neighbors suddenly had the urge to buy the same make and model as you. Those cars have always been there, but you haven't been conscious of them.

That's how I want you to notice the word but. *But* is often the word that precedes an excuse or justification for why we can't do something. Let me give you some examples you may find yourself using before the end of this book.

- "This book is full of examples of people who have overcome difficult experiences, *but* I'm not sure it applies to me."
- "I believe these steps work for people who are disciplined, *but* I struggle with focus and follow-through."
- "I plan to work the process and take the time necessary to walk into my limitless life, *but* you know, sometimes life happens, and even our best plans can change."

Now it's your turn. What is the "but" that has been floating around in your subconscious since you started reading this book? Maybe there are several. What are those hidden excuses that you've already wrestled with? These are limiting beliefs. We need to deal with them before we go any further.

One of the most powerful exercises I use in my coaching practice is to identify the excuses and the justifications that we typically use and literally flush them down the toilet. Here's what I need you to do. Grab a roll of toilet paper and a marker. Write those excuses and justifications on squares of toilet paper. You'll need to examine the buts you have used throughout your life concerning your future and dreams. This may take a little bit of thinking and some space to process. Try writing down every one that comes to mind.

Once you've written them all down, take that roll of toilet paper, tear off the excuses, wad them up, and flush them all down the toilet. Next time those excuses and justifications come up, you can remind yourself that they are no longer a part of who you are. You have wiped yourself clean (pun intended) and are moving forward.

Think about it like this—when using the bathroom, no one, after disposing of the toilet paper, reaches back in the toilet to take it back. OK, OK, I know that's gross, but I promise that you won't forget it, and every time one of those *buts* comes up, you're going to remember flushing your excuses and justifications down the toilet.

If you do not identify and deal with these limiting beliefs at the beginning, then no matter how hard you work at everything else, you will continually find yourself back where you started. You'll spend a lot of time and energy going around the mountain but never going up.

> *The only limits to the possibilities in your life*
> *tomorrow are the buts you use today.*
> —Les Brown

Starting now, no buts allowed!

6

What If My Normal Isn't Normal?

The first step towards getting somewhere is to decide that you are not going to stay where you are.
—John Pierpont Morgan

My son was nine years old and struggling in school. All through his fourth-grade year, Melinda and I had found ourselves meeting with his teachers more often than we had expected. He was struggling to follow directions and stay on task. He was becoming increasingly frustrated about his experience with school and the other kids. We also noticed a change with his gymnastics team. While he was very good at gymnastics, he was increasingly isolated and separated from the rest of the team. Both his teacher and coach shared a similar concern about his ability to focus and pay attention, which was distracting his classmates and teammates.

After one particularly difficult day at school, I found my son crying in the backyard. I asked him what was wrong, and his response broke my heart. "Why am I so different from the rest of the kids? I just want to be normal."

I wish I could tell you that I had the perfect answer, that I told him that he didn't have to be "normal" like the rest of the kids, and he was fine the way he was. But I didn't. At that time, I didn't have an answer for him, and I didn't fully understand why he felt different. I did assure him that he was OK and that we would figure it out.

This led me to a few questions that have become pivotal in my personal growth and a foundational principle of this book. What if our normal isn't normal—it's simply what we've settled for or what others have decided is normal? Who determines normality? Normal can typically be defined as any behavior or condition that is usual, expected, typical, or conforms to a pre-existing standard.[7]   Our current actions, thoughts, and behaviors that play out every day are our normal. This includes the challenges we face and the outcomes we get.

Remember those comfort zones and how "normal" can be a false ceiling over our lives and future? Think about a time you failed at something. Did you say, "That's what I expected" or "That's typical"? Perhaps when things don't work out as you planned, instead of searching for another way forward, you simply think, "I'm not surprised," and move on to the next thing. If so, look back at your life to see if there are areas where you have settled—lowering the bar of expectation. Maybe you used to be a risk-taker and now you don't see the point. Maybe you used to have dreams of a future that now seems like a fantasy.

I like to say, "Normal is the house that limiting beliefs built." Let's deconstruct that house by identifying the limiting beliefs keeping you from a limitless life. This is not an easy task for many of us because these beliefs are hiding deep in the foundation, and we can't imagine living any other way. Because the limited life has become "normal," anything greater seems like something outside of our control.

Limiting beliefs often show up as declarations we make about ourselves and our abilities. Try this simple test to see if you are living with limiting beliefs and settling for a normal that was never supposed to be normal. Have you ever made any of the following statements?

Normal is the house that limiting beliefs built.

- I am not good/smart/strong/pretty/talented enough.
- I don't have enough money/experience/time/friends/ patience.
- I'll never be a great leader.
- I am too old/young to _____.
- I am not worthy of being loved/happy.
- No one ever listens to me.
- I will never be a good husband/wife.
- Life is too hard.
- I am unlucky.
- Change is too hard.
- Bad things always happen to me.
- I am not good with money.
- I will always be alone.
- There is never enough time to _____.
- I don't know where to start.
- Everyone is better than me.
- I never finish what I start.

Maybe you felt frustrated or even a little offended reading over that list. You thought, *This guy has no idea what he's talking about. He doesn't know my life or what I have been through.* You stopped at certain statements and began to justify them. You are telling yourself that it can't be a limiting belief if it is true.

It is important to recognize that there are limitations in the real world—this is when your circumstances really are preventing you from accomplishing your goals. In my experience, however, limiting beliefs keep people bound far more than they realize. This is why I challenge you to look at all of the above statements with a fresh perspective and different questions.

How can you tell the difference between a real limitation and a limiting belief that simply feels real? If the belief involves a physical limitation or a circumstance that is truly outside of your control, then it may be a legitimate limitation. At the end of this process, if you discover that a limiting belief is a true limitation, you can then begin to create a strategy to compensate for it or build around it. And you might be shocked by what you can accomplish even with massive limitations. Take Nick Vujicic, for example—born without arms or legs, today he travels the world as a motivational speaker and evangelist. Oh, and he's an author, musician, and actor who also enjoys fishing, painting, and swimming. Even true limitations don't have to mean settling for a less-than life.

If you discover that your issue is not a true limitation but rather something you have chosen to believe because of people or circumstances, you will soon have a process to crush it, replace it, and rise above it.

Remember, sometimes we hold on to limiting beliefs for so long we don't recognize them as limiting beliefs anymore—we call them normal. We start believing or thinking that we don't have a choice. Life has become something that is happening to us. We stop believing that our lives can make a difference, and we begin to feel stuck, depressed, and frustrated. We believe it's too late to change.

If you honestly can't recognize any limiting beliefs in your mind, consider they may be hidden in areas of your life that you have isolated and minimized. You've closed yourself off from those areas, and you're only focusing on the places where you are most successful.

Be careful not to let success in one area blind you from limiting beliefs in other areas.

Be careful not to let success in one area blind you from limiting beliefs in other areas. Many of us have set up our life in silos; we have taught ourselves not to allow the emotions in one area of our life to bleed into other areas. While this can help us through difficult times, it is not healthy to live there. We were not meant to compartmentalize our feelings.

For some of you, this statement may create some discomfort. You believe that the silos you have created are the only thing that is keeping you moving forward and able to function in any kind of strength and security. You think the silos are your friends, but anything that keeps something out also keeps you locked in and limited.

I once coached a successful businesswoman whom I will call Sherry. She'd reached out to me to help her launch a new business endeavor that she was struggling to bring to fruition. She felt the problem lay in her strategy and was hoping to gain some new insight and perspective on the process.

I quickly realized Sherry was holding onto a limiting belief that was sabotaging her success. The issue was not her strategy—it was her confidence, her belief in herself, and her ability. If you'd talked to Sherry or looked at her life, you would never have questioned her confidence or abilities. She had achieved great success in the companies she had worked with and was engaged in the community, serving on several boards and committees.

Sherry was excellent at working for someone else and helping them achieve their vision and objectives, but she hit a snag when she started working for herself and seeking to make her dreams a reality. She was terrified and lacked confidence in her personal goals.

Once Sherry was able to see these limiting beliefs and recognize the power they had over her, we were able to identify the source of her limiting beliefs and the lies she was believing. You see, Sherry had a very demeaning and verbally abusive father. Nothing she ever did was good enough, and no matter how hard she tried, he always found something to criticize. She had compartmentalized part of her life (created a silo) by burying the experience, telling herself it never happened, and putting her attention on others' dreams while giving up on her own. She thought her limiting beliefs were a fence to protect her, but they became a cage that kept her from growing and pursuing her dreams of one day running her own business.

The problem with compartmentalization is that the negative experiences we're running from don't remain in their silos—they bleed over into every part of our lives. Sherry believed that as long as she stayed away from anything that had to do with her desires, she would never have to face or deal with the limiting beliefs about her own value and competence. The problem was that, deep down, she knew she was created for more. She had longings and desires for something greater. She found herself getting tired and frustrated helping others reach their dreams while burying her own.

When we are living a less-than life, the limitless life that we were born and created for goes unrealized. One of the greatest tragedies we can experience is to come to the end of our lives with those dreams and desires dead within us. Fortunately for Sherry, she was able to recognize the compartment she had built around her experience, and she had the courage to identify the limiting beliefs, find where they came from, and begin to replace them with the truth that reignited the passion and dreams within her.

Whatever your normal is, it does not have to define you and your future. You do not have to remain where you are. But if you want to go up, you must choose to go through. If you are going to live a limitless life, you will need to identify and crush your limiting beliefs. This path is not easy, but I promise it will be worth it.

If you want to change your outcomes, the next step is to identify the source of your limiting beliefs. What were those experiences in your life that contributed to what you believe today? That's the subject of the next chapter.

But before you turn the page, go back and review the limiting belief statements listed above. Grab a pen or highlighter and mark those statements that are familiar, the ones that have found their way into your vocabulary. If you're not sure what statements you use, I invite you to ask a trusted friend to review the list and share with you any of these statements that they have heard you say. Make a list of these statements; we will come back to them in the next two chapters.

7

Life Happens

Challenges are what make life interesting.
Overcoming them is what makes life meaningful.
—Ralph Waldo Emmerson

E very experience in your life, good or bad, has marked you in some way. If I asked you to go back over your life and identify the most important markers, could you? The strange thing about this exercise is that we typically don't have a hard time remembering the negative experiences, but often the positive ones seem to escape us.

As part of my mindset coaching, I ask my clients to come up with one hundred positive "I am" declarations. Typically, they have no problem with the first twenty to thirty words, but after that, the struggle begins. On the other hand, it's easy to recall negative experiences and list negative declarations. Our brains seem to be wired toward the negative, not the positive.

In his book *Hardwiring Happiness*, Rick Hanson explains that the brain is like Velcro for negative experiences but Teflon for positive ones. This is one of the challenges with moving from limiting beliefs to limitless beliefs. As humans, we are all prone to what is called negativity bias.

Negativity bias refers to our proclivity to attend to, learn from, and use negative information far more than positive information.[8] It has been shown that negative events elicit more rapid and more prominent responses than non-negative events.[9] The result is an unhealthy sense of fear, anxiety, and depression.

Research suggests that, because of this negativity bias, it takes five positive experiences to counteract one negative experience.[10] While this can feel overwhelming and nearly impossible to overcome, there is hope. While it will take intentionality and consistent, focused effort, getting out of our negative thinking is possible.

In this chapter, we're going to look at the three major kinds of experiences that can establish limiting beliefs. As you read, take a moment to reflect and identify these events in your life. Doing the hard work of discovery here could mean the difference between walking in the limitless life you were created for and walking in the limited life you are settling for.

> **Doing the hard work of discovery here could mean the difference between walking in the limitless life you were created for and walking in the limited life you are settling for.**

The Familiar

Some "life happens" moments are so small we don't notice them passing us by. Have you ever been driving for a long time, and it's almost like you lose consciousness? You find yourself at your desired destination, but you can't remember how you got there. It's always in familiar territory, a place you've driven so many times before that you no longer have to think about it.

Repetition is a powerful tool. When we experience something or hear the same words many times, it impacts what we believe and how we think at a subconscious level. Often the words we most frequently hear come not from an outside source but rather from the inner dialogue that goes on in our heads. When a steady flow of negative self-talk becomes so routine that we no longer challenge it, we generate limiting beliefs in that area.

Negative experiences aren't the only kind that mark us—positive events also shape the lenses we use to view life. While these positive experiences don't leave us with limiting beliefs, they can often lead us to a comfort/danger zone. Throughout this process, we must be willing to look at both the positive and the negative experiences from our past, asking ourselves how these experiences are showing up or serving us in our present.

The One-Off Comment

The second kind of experience that creates limiting beliefs is the one-off comment. One word from a friend or a seemingly trivial event can have a profound impact. I've found that one-off experiences are often the most dangerous. The behaviors and limiting beliefs that we adopt because of one-off comments are the hardest to recognize and, therefore, the last to be crushed and replaced.

My son has a passion for music. He is a self-taught guitar player and has been writing and playing since he was nine years old. Music was his therapy as he was going through the challenges of life. As he got older and entered his twenties, his passion to pursue music full-time grew. The challenge with a music career is the inconsistency in shows and pay as you're getting started. There's also a lot of risk involved, and it can be scary stepping into the unknown.

As I was talking to my son about some of his frustrations in pursuit of his music career, I asked him what his biggest challenge (other than money) was. He proceeded to tell me the story of an experience he'd had with a family member almost three years earlier. At that time, he was beginning to pursue shows and gigs consistently. He was excited about the possibilities and shared his excitement with a family member whom he respects and who has always been an important influence in his life. After sharing all that he was doing, the first response my son got from this family member was, "Don't quit your day job."

This family member meant well, loves my son greatly, and has always encouraged and believed in him. The comment was not meant to be a discouragement; it was simply a statement from a perspective that places a high value on security and consistency. This family member never gave it another thought, but it stuck with my son and marked him. Three years later, he could recall this two-minute conversation and how deeply it had impacted him. The narrative he created from that statement was that this family member did not believe in him and didn't believe he should pursue a music career. That was the farthest thing from the truth, but it demonstrates how five small words can change someone's beliefs and behaviors.

The Decisions of Others

The last type of experience involves choices that were made for you—decisions you had no say in. These experiences typically come from those close to us—parents, guardians, and family members who believe they know what is best for us.

This next story is a little harder for me to share because it impacted me and my family in some very challenging ways. We have overcome the effects of this decision my wife and I made, but not without some cost and a lot of therapy along the way.

I have shared some of this journey with you already, but as a quick reminder, my wife and I have two amazing, talented children we had the honor and privilege of adopting at birth. While we are huge supporters of adoption, we did not start off understanding all the dynamics that surround adoptive families. My son struggled through his teenage years with a lot of anger, intense emotions about his adoption, and a search for identity and independence, along with the normal process of going through puberty. On top of this, we discovered he struggled with ADD and ADHD. His relationships became a challenge until school was no longer a safe place. No matter how hard we tried to understand and help, things kept spiraling out of control. As a family, we engaged in counseling, shifted to homeschooling, and spent a lot of time in prayer. We could feel things coming to a head but were at a loss to help my son and our family through this difficult time.

My son would often express how he hated his life and everyone around him and wished that it would all simply end. We saw this as a cry for help but thought we had it under control until one evening, in a fit of rage, he seemed to cross the line into suicidal ideation. We realized we were in over our heads and were desperate to find help. Ten days later, my son and I were on a plane heading to a boarding school on the East Coast. It was the hardest decision we have ever made, and we felt like complete failures. We were sending our son away because we no longer believed we could help him through all that he was experiencing.

I'll never forget driving off with my son cursing us and turning his back on us as we drove away. Even sharing this with you over ten years later, I can still feel the pain of that moment. There is so much more to this story that will ultimately find its way into another book, but let me conclude this story on a positive note. While that decision marked our son and our entire family, redemption, and healing did come. The first boarding school experience did not end well, but the second one became the foundation for hope and healing. If you ask my son about it today, he will tell you that the decision to go to the second boarding school saved his life.

This experience, while ultimately positive, created some limiting beliefs for my son as well as my daughter. This was one of those situations where choices were made for them that they had no control over. While this may be an extreme example, you have had decisions made for you that might have been for your good, but at the time, they did not feel like it. They marked you with thoughts and beliefs that have impacted how you view your life, relationships, and even your future.

Victim to Victor

Remember what we're doing in this section: honestly assessing your current reality and setting the dot on the GPS that says, "You are here." When you understand where you have come from and where you are, you can choose where you are going and how you want to get there.

> What if these things didn't happen to me, but they actually happened for me?

If you could map the journey of your life up to this point, you would discover a series of incredible adventures with some extreme highs and lows. One of my coaches offered me this thought when I got stuck in a pity party about all the things that I have experienced in my life. He suggested I take a different perspective and ask the question, "What if these things didn't happen *to* me, but they actually happened *for* me?"

To be honest, I didn't like that question at all. But as I reflected on it, I saw the power in shifting my perspective. When I saw things as happening for me, I moved away from the victim mentality and took back control, adopting a victor mentality. I began to see every experience, challenge, setback, and gut punch as an opportunity to learn, grow, and overcome.

In the end, it doesn't matter how you got to where you are. The question becomes, *do you want to remain there?* I won't blame you if you answer yes. Sometimes, it's easier to remain where we are and accept our fate, making the most of the situation we find ourselves in. If this is where you find yourself, I understand, but may I challenge you with another thought?

As I am approaching life in my sixties, I've begun to realize that the days in front of me are much shorter than the days behind me. I'm asking myself questions like, "Has my life mattered? Have I made a difference? What kind of influence have I had on the people in my life?" What I'm searching for is my legacy. Legacy for me is not about being remembered— it's about the positive impact of my life rippling into the world around me. I don't want to leave the legacy of a victim, someone who let life happen to him.

In the previous chapter, I asked you to begin to identify limiting beliefs in your life. These beliefs often show up as statements. Those statements come from beliefs you hold, and those beliefs were shaped by how you interpreted your experiences. Before leaving this chapter, spend a few minutes reviewing those statements and asking yourself two questions:

- How do these statements show up in my life?
- What is the context or source of each one?

You may discover that the context or source is similar for several of the statements.

I have found it virtually impossible to change someone's outcomes sustainably without recognizing how they got to where they are. In the final chapter of this section, I will introduce you to what I call the Born Limitless Framework. The framework is true in all our lives. When we understand the framework, we begin to see how our beliefs are formed and our behaviors are created. This is a critical step for growth and the dicovery of the limitless life you were born for.

8

The Born Limitless Framework

External circumstances will not change until
internal belief systems change.
—Dr. Myles Munroe

Y ou're probably beginning to see a pattern by now, the framework of sorts. All experiences, both positive and negative, typically trigger an innate or raw emotion. That emotion triggers a physiological response that we interpret or define in terms of a feeling. As we interpret and define the feeling and its source, we begin to form thoughts and opinions that lead to a belief. Beliefs drive our behaviors, or as I often say, how we believe directly impacts how we be*live*. Ultimately, your behaviors produce your outcomes.

This is what I refer to as the Born Limitless Framework. When we understand the framework and how it works, we can deconstruct the process, reframe experiences, identify limiting beliefs, and begin replacing those beliefs, creating new behaviors and producing better outcomes.

The Born Limitless Framework

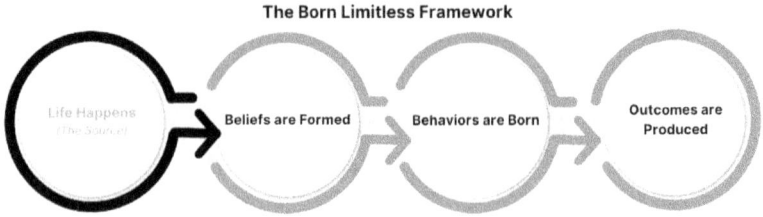

When you are unsatisfied with the outcomes in your life, what is your first response? You probably try to change your behavior. What you might have discovered is that your ability to change your behavior and sustain that change is largely dependent on the strength of your will. When the challenges come and "life happens," your first response is to revert to old behaviors, your comfort zones. This typically leads to great frustration, and you give up trying because the new behaviors you've tried to implement are unsustainable. You're back where you started—but, if you're honest, it feels as though you're even farther away.

Here's the gold nugget of truth, the key to your future success and the transformation you need to walk out the limitless life you were born and created for. You may want to highlight this next statement and dog-ear the page.

Are you ready? Don't miss it.

If you want to change your outcomes, you don't start by changing your behavior. You must first identify the belief that formed the behavior and change the belief.

Here is another way to look at this.

- Different outcomes require different behaviors.
- Different behaviors require different decisions.
- Different decisions require different thoughts.
- Different thoughts require different beliefs.

Let me be clear: I am not saying we should not attempt to create new behaviors. If we want different outcomes, our behaviors will have to change. But, changing our behaviors without addressing the beliefs that drive them will rarely, if ever, lead to sustained change.

Regardless of how we look at the process, everything begins with what we believe. This is simple but not easy. You must put in the hard work of identifying the limiting beliefs you are holding and the source and context in which they were born. Once you can identify both your limiting belief and its source, you can begin to do the deep work of change that leads to transformation.

I know that limiting beliefs can be powerful and hard to uproot. Let me share a personal story of how limiting beliefs can impact our decisions and keep us from blessings if they are not identified and dealt with.

Do you remember my story about the encounter with my babysitter in fourth grade? It was one of those "life happens" moments I had no control over and did nothing to deserve. That experience led to the formation of some powerful and damaging beliefs that created behaviors and actions that almost cost me one of my greatest blessings.

I was a "runner" for much of my young life. Not the athletic kind of runner—the kind that never finished what he started. I held a limiting belief that I was not very smart and would never amount to anything, but I hid it by creating a mask of strength and confidence. As far as appearances went, I was smart and could do anything. The truth is I was scared to death that if I stayed anywhere long enough, I would be found out as a fraud. Deep down, I knew I wasn't who others thought I was. I would always do just enough to gain people's confidence, but when it was time to step up, I found a way to excuse myself. I would end the relationship, take a new job, or even go so far as to move to another town.

I finally had to face my fears after I left everything in Indianapolis to move to Houston, chasing a girl who challenged me to think bigger and be better. I'll never forget the day I woke up with an overwhelming thought in my head: "I can't do this anymore. It's time to run." I had won over her family and her friends, everyone thought I was a good person and perfect for her. The pressure had built, and I knew if I didn't do something soon, they would discover I was not the person I had presented to them. The challenge was that I truly loved and cared for this girl.

As I contemplated how I would get out of the relationship, a crazy thought came into my head and heart—what if, instead of running, I proposed and we got married? I know, romantic, isn't it? I remember the conversation I had in my mind. Instead of saying, "I can't do this," I said, "I can."

I got up the next morning and drove to her father's house to ask him if I could marry his daughter. After getting his blessing, I drove to Baybrook Mall, walked into Kay Jewelers, and found a ring I liked at a price I couldn't afford. I proceeded to call my bank, and they faxed over the loan papers. I completed them and faxed them back, and thirty minutes later, I was approved for enough money to purchase the ring, plus $500. I decided to use that $500 to buy a registered kitten at the pet store near the mall exit. My girlfriend loved cats, and I thought it would be a great way to propose.

Even when we recognize them and know them to be untrue, limiting beliefs can be incredibly powerful. Back at home, I placed the cat under the sink in the guest bathroom, and Melinda and I went out to dinner. During dinner, I proceeded to sabotage the entire night. The way I behaved was calculated to get us into an argument. I could see what I was doing, yet I could not stop it.

The drive back to the house was long and quiet. By now, I figured the cat had either destroyed the bathroom or was running loose in the house, or it was dead. Everything was falling apart. Once we got to the house, I went straight to the bathroom, and fortunately, the kitten was fine. I sat on the toilet holding the kitten for the next thirty minutes, wrestling with the choice to stay or to run.

One thing I knew was that I was tired of running. The other thing that was going through my mind was a scripture verse. A few months earlier, I had decided to make Jesus Christ my Lord and Savior. One of the scriptures that led me to that decision was Jeremiah 29:11—"'For I know the plans I have for you,' declares the Lord, 'plans to prosper you and not to harm you, plans to give you hope and a future.'" As I sat there holding the kitten, I thought, *If God's plans are for my good and my future, then why am I so afraid?*

I walked out of the bathroom and over to Melinda, got on my knees, and asked her to forgive me for the way I'd acted at the restaurant. Then I gave her the kitten with the ring attached to the collar and asked her to marry me. That was the moment I chose to face my limiting belief, admit it was not true, and embrace a new belief and a new truth.

The first few years of marriage were difficult, and I would be lying if I said there were not moments when I felt like running and giving up, but I pressed in and pushed through; my faith had a lot to do with it. That was over thirty-two years ago, and Melinda and I are more in love today than we have ever been.

How you choose to write on the remaining pages of your life's book has everything to do with how you respond to those experiences in your journey when "life happened." The beliefs you develop from those experiences will either be the source of your bondage or the path to your freedom.

The beliefs you develop from those experiences will either be the source of your bondage or the path to your freedom.

You are about to experience the Pivot. You will have to answer the question, "Is my current reality as good as it gets, or do I believe there is more?" Actions follow beliefs. This is where the transformation and growth will happen. It is where new beliefs collide with new behaviors.

Let's see if you are ready to move forward:

- Are you willing to acknowledge where you are and how you feel right now?
- Are you willing to acknowledge that your "normal" is holding you back?
- Are you willing to take an honest look at how you got here and the limiting beliefs that you have adopted along the way?

If you answered yes, then you're ready to continue. Say this declaration out loud:

**I choose the limitless life I was born and created for.
My current reality will not define my future possibilities.
I choose to grow!**

As we move into the next section, embrace the discomfort and stretching you are bound to experience. This will require making a mental shift from the belief that things are going to become easier to the truth that things will probably get harder and more challenging first. Here is another key principle I want you to grab hold of as we move forward: *you must learn to do hard things better.* If you are thinking that your life will suddenly become easier as a result of this process, you are setting yourself up for more pain and failure.

One of my son's counselors at boarding school helped him—and me—understand that the struggles we experience in life are inevitable; they will come. The challenge is not that we go through struggles, the challenge is that we have never learned to struggle well. The choice I am asking you to make is to learn how to struggle well. You must choose to be stronger than your limiting beliefs. They will not go away if you do not choose discomfort and challenge them. No one can choose this path for you. You will have to face the excuses and justifications that are hiding deep in your subconscious, waiting for your permission to lock you down and keep you bound in your less-than life.

Quick—what are the excuses that come to mind right now? What are the first thoughts you have when you think about identifying, facing, and crushing your limiting beliefs and the places of comfort in your life? Those first thoughts of your subconscious mind are powerful. Take a minute and write them down no matter how bizarre, crazy, or irrelevant they might seem. The transformation begins when you permit yourself to challenge the status quo of your life. There is an untapped, limitless potential within you waiting for you to release it in your life. From this moment on, choose to focus your attention and energy on where you are headed rather than where you have been. What you give attention and energy to will grow.

I love this quotation from Doreen Virtue: "Anything that you fight with or struggle against grows larger. You give power to lower energies by focusing upon them. You don't eliminate darkness by arguing with it. The only way to eliminate darkness is to turn on a light."

It's time to turn on the light and pivot!

The Pivot

Action follows belief. You cannot make a pivot in your life
until you change what you believe.
—Sam Silverstein

I played basketball all through high school and college, and I remember coaching my son at the YMCA when he was five years old. If you've ever had the pleasure of watching a five-year-old play basketball, you've realized that dribbling and passing the ball are not as easy as one might think. One of the first things that basketball coaches teach kids is how to pivot. A good pivot allows you to get away from the defender and create space to pass or shoot. The power of the pivot is in the anchor foot. Once you establish the pivot, you create opportunities for success.

You are about to make a pivot. I encourage you to anchor yourself in your current reality and then pivot away from where you have been and toward your future. When you choose to pivot, you are declaring that your circumstances are not the end of your story. Your future is a blank page; it hasn't happened yet. I hope you can feel the power in that statement, so I am going to repeat it. *Your future is a blank page.* You are both the author and hero. If you want to feel the power of this statement, I encourage you to make it personal and declare it out loud before you move on.

My future is a blank page.
I am the author and hero of my story.

Imagine your life as a book, and the only chapters written so far are the chapters of yesterday. Those chapters help you define the context of today, but they do not determine the chapters of tomorrow. Your past does not decide your future—you do. The only question is how you will choose to define it.

You were created for more! Remember, the *more* we are talking about is not stuff, accomplishments, or titles. It is the influence and impact your life is meant to have on the people and world around you. If you take time to reflect, challenge your current reality, and dream about your preferred future, you will open the door to the limitless life you were created for.

This is why I created The Limitless Leader Blank Page, a five-day challenge to discover the more that you were born and created for. Hundreds of people have experienced this challenge and seen their lives drastically changed. As part of the challenge, they took back control of their future and stopped letting the pains of yesterday influence and impact the potential of tomorrow. If you want to learn more about The Power of a Blank Page, you can find information on my website:

RickTorrison.com/LimitlessLeaderChallenge

For too long, we have allowed the unexpected and unwanted parts of life to impact and influence our perspective.

Remember, the experiences of your life are real, and the feelings that stem from those experiences are real, but you must ask yourself, "Are those experiences based on truth, and do they have to define my current reality and determine my future success?"

How do we get to the more, that limitless life we were born and created for? How do we clean our lenses so that we can have a clear vision of where we are going? How do we identify and crush the limiting beliefs that have kept us living a l ess-than life? To get to the more and embrace the fact that we were born limitless, we must deal with our beliefs and their sources, remove them, and replace them with a new truth. As you begin to embrace and believe the truth, your behaviors and actions will follow. *This is the process of real transformation.*

As we come to a jump stop and plant our foot to make the pivot, I want to cast a vision of what is waiting for you. People use the word transformation often, and it can become watered down and lose its true impact. There is a scripture that speaks powerfully to this idea of transformation. In Romans 12:2, we read, "Do not conform to the pattern of this world but be transformed by the renewing of your mind."

What we know in our minds to be true forms a conviction in our hearts, and that conviction in our hearts translates into action. Therefore, we must first renew our minds. The renewing of our minds—identifying and crushing limiting beliefs and recognizing and eliminating their sources—is the foundation and the beginning of transformation.

I want you to see yourself as a caterpillar going through metamorphosis. Unlocking the limitless life is not simply about cleaning up old mindsets, beliefs, and habits. This process is about the old mindsets, beliefs, and habits dying so that something new can be born. When the butterfly breaks free from the chrysalis, there is no trace of the caterpillar. The limited life of the caterpillar—relegated to slow, methodical movement and easily preyed upon by other insects and animals—has given way to the beauty and majesty of the butterfly. No longer constrained by its old form and limitations, the butterfly is now free to fly, explore new places, and display its beauty to the world. I understand this next statement may sound a little corny, but I believe it to be true. You are that butterfly. The process we will walk through in this last section is the process of metamorphosis. It may be ugly, and some things will have to die, but the new life, that limitless life we've been talking about, will be awakened and released.

Real transformation can only come from the place of revelation. It's that "aha moment" we have all experienced when something we've heard a million times suddenly makes sense. I hope you have had several of those experiences as you have been reading this book. What is one truth that you can begin to embrace today?

This is the process of real transformation and the doorway to the limitless life you were born and created for.

SECTION 3

LIMITLESS

One of the many jobs I had early in my marriage was that of a school bus driver. How I ever qualified for a CDL, I will never know. If you ask my wife, she will tell you that I have a lead foot. Somehow, I always manage to exceed the speed limit without really trying. This is not a good habit when you're driving a school bus full of children.

Fortunately for me and the children, the school bus was equipped with a governor. A governor is a device that controls a vehicle's maximum speed. In this situation, a governor is a good thing. In our personal lives, however, the limiting beliefs that we operate under act as a governor, keeping us from reaching our potential and experiencing a limitless life.

In this final section, we will begin recognizing and releasing our limitless life by identifying, crushing, and replacing our limiting beliefs. This process can transform you to the core. As we walk through it together, we will be removing the governor over your life. Once you understand the process, you can engage the Born Limitless Framework at any time, in any situation.

As you embark on this journey, I want to be clear about expectations going forward. As I mentioned earlier, it is simple but not easy. I will give you the tools and the opportunity to make the shift from information to revelation. In that place of revelation, you will begin to experience true transformation from your limited life to a limitless life.

Before you move forward, you must decide it's time to make a change and choose to do the hard work of transformation. I believe you have already made that choice because you're still here; you're still reading. You've made it through the hardest part—you've allowed me to challenge your current reality and push some buttons that you had hidden or forgotten even existed. You've allowed me to stir up some things that you had hoped were gone but, in truth, were only lying dormant, waiting for the next trigger to set you off and set you back.

There is something magical and powerful about bringing things into the light that strips them of their power. It's only when those things remain in the hidden places that they can have control over your life.

When we acknowledge limiting beliefs, name them, and declare them out loud, we take the first step toward crushing them and replacing them with something new and true. When we do, we shift our foundation, which gives us the opportunity for our greatest growth. Notice I said, "gives us the opportunity"—everything is a choice you must make, and no one can make it for you. You're standing in that choice right now. You have stepped off the shifting sand and onto the rock, and now it's time to start building, growing, and becoming who you were born and created to be. I don't know about you, but I'm excited.

9

Consider the Source

We are products of our past,
but we don't have to be prisoners of it.
—Rick Warren, *The Purpose Driven Life*

You've probably heard the statement, "Consider the source." We have talked about the source as that place where "life happens," and it is the key to our sustained freedom and transformation. It is not uncommon to have both positive and negative sources in our lives at the same time. Some give strength and confidence that lead to our growth, but there are sources that challenge our confidence, feed our fears, and lead to a limited life.

Every belief comes from a source. There is an origination point—something that happened, something that was said, or something we experienced—that ultimately became the source of the belief that we now hold. If you're finding it difficult to wrap your mind around what that looks like, this chapter is for you. I'll walk you through the Born Limitless Framework using parts of my own story so that you can see yourself and your story more clearly.

I recently started going to the gym—not for the first time. After years of failing to reach my health goals, I knew I needed to do something different if I was going to make any progress, so I hired a trainer to help me build a program and stay consistent. One of my objectives was to build strength. My trainer has taught me that you can't add muscle without trauma. To stimulate muscle growth, you must break down muscle tissue, and that forces the muscle to restructure and grow back stronger and bigger than before. In other words, you must deconstruct your current muscle structure to grow it into the new structure that you desire.

I had started and stopped diet and exercise plans in the past with little or no sustained change, and I finally realized that my will to do and be better was strong but not strong enough. There had to be another path forward. What was I doing wrong? Why couldn't I stick to a plan? Then I decided to apply everything I'd learned about the Born Limitless Framework to my health issues, and I discovered that I needed to address the beliefs behind my failure to follow through. Once I addressed the limiting beliefs, I was able to begin the process of tearing down and building back up.

That is a vivid picture of this process of transformation and stepping into the limitless life. It often begins with a deconstruction, recognizing that where we are is not where we want to be and then breaking down how we got here in order to move forward. To stimulate the growth we desire, we often have to tear a few things apart. It can be painful at first, but the new growth and strength is worth it. At the time of writing this book, I have been in the gym for ten months at least four days a week. I wish I had a picture to show you the transformation, but you will have to take my wife's words for it. When I asked her to describe the difference between now and last year, she said I went from "OK" to "hot and sexy." Her words, not mine.

Let's look at the Framework again:

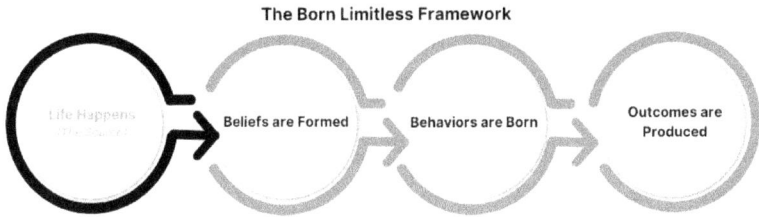

The Born Limitless Framework

Life Happens — Beliefs are Formed — Behaviors are Born — Outcomes are Produced

The process of working through this formula will look different for everyone. It's not linear, and it can be entered into at any point. What is most important is that we do not skip a part of the process but rather deal with each piece. You may easily recognize an undesirable outcome and begin from there. Regarding my health, that's where I started last year when I honestly looked in the mirror. I knew I did not like what I saw, and a recent doctor visit reinforced this by diagnosing me with high cholesterol and prediabetes. The combination of these factors created an awareness of my current condition and an associated feeling of fear. This started my process toward change.

But you don't have to start there—you may be aware of your undesirable behaviors and actions (like my terrible eating habits and lazy lifestyle) without connecting them to real outcomes. Other people are extremely self-aware and can easily identify their source and places of trauma but are unable to identify the limiting beliefs that have taken root. What I have learned in coaching people through this process is that the hardest place to start is with our beliefs. No one wants to challenge their beliefs initially because this can be a very humbling experience. To challenge our beliefs, we must admit that they are wrong or faulty and are not serving us. This is not always the easiest place to start, but can ultimately be the most powerful.

As one of my coaches once told me, don't begin with the hardest things, start with something easy and create wins. Those wins build confidence and allow you to get to the deep and difficult things. As you work through this process, let me suggest you start with something that is already on the surface and is fairly easy to identify and engage. Keeping it simple as you begin will allow you to experience success. Once you learn this process and experience success and freedom in this surface area, you can apply it to deeper areas and stronger limiting beliefs.

If finding a starting point isn't so easy for you, go back to Chapter Six, where I listed a series of statements to help you identify limiting beliefs. Which one stands out to you or elicits the strongest emotion when you think about it? Once you've identified that statement or a series of statements around a similar topic, I want you to ask the next question: "How do these statements play out in the choices that I make?" In other words, "How do these beliefs impact my behaviors?" Remember, these are called limiting beliefs for a reason. In this process, it is important to remember there is another belief that is greater and does not limit you but sets you free. This is the belief we are contending for.

Years ago, I went through this exact exercise myself. I looked at my list, and there were several statements that I could easily group together. They formed a singular belief which led me to repeated outcomes that were less than what I felt was possible. I accepted this belief as normal, and it became my ceiling.

The statements that I grouped included "I will never be successful," "I don't deserve to be successful," "No one will listen to me," "There are people better than me," "I am not good with money," and "I have tried this before." As I walked through all these statements, I realized they had at least one thing in common—they all spoke to my lack of confidence and belief in myself and my ability to ever make a difference in the world around me. I could summarize all the statements with one simple belief: I am not worthy, and my current reality is as good as it will ever be.

This belief impacted my confidence and led me to settle. It was not a conscious belief that I could identify when I was living it out, but I experienced the effects emotionally, which impacted my behaviors and outcomes. The power that drives this process is found in the associated emotions. The danger is not that we have emotions that elicit feelings but rather how we interpret or define those feelings. How we interpret our feelings becomes part of the cycle that will either keep us locked up or propel us to greater growth and freedom. Emotions are real, but they are not always based on truth.

Once you've identified these statements and how they have impacted and shaped your beliefs, you'll start to see how they influence the behaviors and outcomes you have experienced throughout your life. One of the ways this lack of confidence showed up for me was in overcompensation—a false appearance of confidence—which led me to become a "runner" (and nearly lose the love of my life, as I shared earlier). My running put a ceiling on my life and what I believed I could achieve. I started settling and making excuses for why I wasn't more successful. My freedom began when I acknowledged my limiting belief and began to root out the source.

Remember where we started. These beliefs and accompanying behaviors that are producing a less-than life come from a source. Sustained freedom can be difficult if not impossible to achieve if the source is not identified and dealt with. This can become a very interesting and tricky process.

A source feeds us and anchors us to itself. If it is a positive source, it leads to our growth. If it is a negative source, it acts as a ceiling over our lives. The sources we are seeking to identify are the ones that are keeping us from our limitless lives. Don't underestimate the power of a source. If we don't do the work to discover it and uproot it, it becomes like a weed in the garden—we keep breaking off the stem but never deal with the root, and the weed lives on.

As you follow me on this process to identify, crush, and replace your limiting beliefs, don't be afraid to feel your emotions in the process. If you don't engage your feelings and redefine them, your actions will become robotic and unsustainable. The key is not to get stuck in your feelings but to move through them, identifying which are based on lies and replacing them with the truth.

It is important to mention here that there are also sources that come from a deeper trauma than we may be willing to acknowledge. This trauma may require more professional help than this book can offer. What is important is that you recognize the different sources that are impacting your growth and future and that you dare to make the decisions necessary for you to experience freedom. Seeking professional help in the area of our mental health and beliefs is not a sign of weakness; it is a sign of great strength as we become jealous of our own growth and the limitless life waiting for us.

If you find yourself struggling to identify your source, it often helps to ask the question, "When do I first remember experiencing these thoughts or feeling this way?" I refer to this as the point of first remembrance. Maybe it was an experience on the playground as a child, a comment from a stranger in the grocery store, or something you overheard others talking about. Many different types of source experiences seem trivial at the time and yet mark us and influence how we think and what we believe.

Don't underestimate the power of subtle source experiences. Although I don't remember much about living in Franklin Park (a suburb of Chicago), I do remember my second-grade class. I don't remember the teacher, I don't remember any of the students, I only remember having to sit in the corner of the room in a chair facing the wall and wearing a pointed paper hat with the word *dunce* written on it. I don't even remember why I got in trouble or what caused me to have to sit in that seat. What's interesting about this experience is that I did not remember it until I was working through some of my insecurities and the beliefs I had about my intelligence and ability to be successful. I could not trace a person to the belief, but as I processed, I began remembering different moments when I was made to feel inferior or less-than.

The second example also happened when I was young. Remember, I was raised by my mom, grandmother, and hippie uncle, and I realized I was different from my friends who had stable, "normal" families. One day, a friend asked, "Where is your dad?" No one had ever asked me that before. But at that moment, I knew that I had to make up a story. I couldn't admit to them that I didn't have a dad or that my mom wasn't married. For some reason, that felt wrong. So I made up a story about my dad being killed in the Vietnam War. And that was the last of the questions. This response started a journey of lies and exaggerations about my life and my identity.

I share these two stories with you because both of them played a significant role in the limiting beliefs I developed over my life. They weren't associated with a person or a traumatic action or experience. I know the dunce cap sounds pretty traumatic, but back then, it was normal for the "problem" children to be labeled and set aside. Others didn't seem shocked by it, and no one stood up and shouted that it was wrong.

The source of our limiting beliefs can come from anywhere, at any time, and at any age. A limiting belief is something that we believe about ourselves that puts a limit on what we think is possible, who we can become, and what we can accomplish. We often use our limiting beliefs as a shield or protective mechanism to keep us from doing hard things, taking risks, or stepping outside our comfort zone. We've convinced ourselves that it's easier to live with the limiting belief than to attempt something that we might fail at.

Identifying a source can be a little scary. What if you discover it is a beloved family member or friend or a situation that you caused yourself? Don't worry, we will discuss those situations in the next chapter.

We've covered a lot of ground in this chapter, so I'll summarize. The truth is we all suffer from limiting beliefs. Each of our limiting beliefs comes from a source, and that source may be in the form of people or experiences, a singular moment, or a collection of statements made over time. How we interpret or define that source experience will determine the beliefs that we adopt. If we interpret or define the source experience negatively, we form limiting beliefs. On the other hand, if we can reframe and see those source experiences as moments of learning and growth, then instead of limiting beliefs, we create limitless beliefs and opportunities.

Can I challenge you to take a step forward? If you have identified different sources in your life, take as much time as you need and begin to reframe them. Instead of seeing yourself in the scene, place yourself outside of the scene and look for things you can learn. Begin to reframe and redefine the source experience. Instead of the pain, see the potential. See it as a foundation under your feet, and begin to build new beliefs on it.

10

Cut the Cord

You cannot sleep with the enemy and be successful. . . .
Every cord that binds you to failure, every cord that binds
you to fear, you gotta cut it!
—Eric Thomas

I n my personal experience and after walking people through the Born Limitless Framework, I have discovered that, in many cases, our limiting beliefs come from source experiences involving loved ones or friends. Because this can be one of the hardest areas to deal with, I wanted to take time to unpack this process and show how you can reframe your relationships.

When dealing with these sources, you may discover many different emotions. This is often where people get bogged down and are afraid to move forward. The hardest source to identify is the one that is closest to us, someone we have trusted. If this is the case for you, this next statement is extremely important—identifying your source as someone whom you love or value does not mean that you have to judge them as a bad person, break your relationship with them, or confront them. While this may be necessary in some situations, it is not the starting point. Remember, the goal is your freedom and moving into the limitless life that you were born and created for. The power of the process is in identifying the source and the belief that was born from it. It is possible to identify the lie tied to the limiting belief and reject it without having to reject the source.

Sometimes, we discover that we are the source—our limiting belief comes from something that we did or said. Identifying ourselves as the source can be scary. It requires an honest assessment that may reveal things in ourselves we have been covering up. It is important that we reject the belief and not reject ourselves by adding more guilt or self-criticism.

> **It is possible to identify the lie tied to the limiting belief and reject it without having to reject the source.**

We can do this in a process that I call reframing. When we recognize the negative impact of how we received and defined a comment or experience, we can reframe the context and our interpretation or definition of the experience. This does not justify or dismiss hurtful or untrue things that were done or said to us, but it does allow us to place them in a larger and broader context.

One aspect that impacts our ability to experience freedom from these limiting beliefs involves intent. Negative source experiences can be intentional or unintentional. While one is easier to forgive and address than the other, both are damaging and contribute to the limiting beliefs that we may hold over our lives.

Let me first address those actions that we believe were intentional or premeditated. These typically produce the greatest amount of trauma, and they may require you to reach out for professional support and help in processing. Oftentimes, we repress these experiences because of the pain associated with them, which makes identifying the limiting beliefs difficult.

If you have been the recipient of verbal, physical, and/or emotional abuse and trauma in the past, it is important that you hear this: Nothing you have experienced at the hands of someone else is your fault. Even if you have acted in ways that may have contributed to someone else's actions, you did not force someone to say or do something against you. They are 100 percent responsible for their choices and the actions that they took—just as you are 100 percent responsible for the choices and actions that you take in response. This revelation is powerful because it also gives you the total ability to make a new choice, embrace a new belief, and move in a new direction. I'm not implying that this is easy; what I am saying is that it is possible. Taking responsibility is at the heart of reframing.

If you are currently a recipient of ongoing verbal, physical, and or emotional abuse and trauma, it is important that you hear this: You do not deserve it, it is not your fault, and you do not have to remain where you are. I understand this is easier said than done. One of the first steps in your freedom is believing that you deserve better and that you are not the source or cause of the abuse that you are under. When you walk away from the abuse, you are not automatically walking away from the abuser, although that may be necessary. Walking away from the abuse can often lead the abuser to reassess their actions and get the help they need.

It is time that you became jealous for your freedom and your future. It is time you became your top priority and began making decisions with your best interest in mind. You are worth it. You are courageous. You are not alone. Self-condemnation, guilt, and shame are not yours to carry, and they are not your path to freedom. They are the bars of the prison that is keeping you from the limitless life and the *more* you were born and created for.

In this situation, you must physically separate yourself from the negative source, even if only temporarily, so that you can do the work in your life necessary to set a new foundation and allow yourself to move forward. In extreme cases, you may need to involve a third party. The most important thing for you to hear is that you are not the cause of what is happening to you, but you can be the one who says enough. When the source of our limiting beliefs and the trauma in our lives comes from those close to us, we must choose to pivot away from the reality we are living in toward a new reality and future that is waiting for us.

In my work as a coach, I have discovered that many of us spend a ton of attention, emotion, energy, and resources on things we can't control. I want to help you focus your efforts on what you can control, those things that make a difference in your pursuit of a limitless life. You can control how you choose to respond to your life experiences and the people behind them. In some situations, there is no other way to move toward freedom without cutting yourself off from a relationship completely. But for many of us, that is not an option, so we must find a way to emotionally separate ourselves and the limiting beliefs that we hold from the source without physically separating ourselves from the source. It is possible, though not easy.

Let me share an analogy that may help you understand what you need to do and why. Think about the connection between your source experience and your current mindset or beliefs as an umbilical cord. The umbilical cord's purpose is to transport energy from the source (mother) to feed the child. That energy can be positive (healthy) or negative (unhealthy). The negative energy from your limiting belief comes from a source, and the only way to stop the flow is to cut the cord. Once the cord is cut, you can reframe your beliefs and begin engaging in new behaviors.

It is important to remember that cutting the umbilical cord does not necessarily mean that you cut your relationship with the source. It simply means you no longer receive the negative energy that the connection was feeding you. Once the negative source is removed, you need to replace it with a new, positive source or narrative. Again, this is where reframing is so powerful.

If you can cut the cord from a source who is also a loved one or a friend, you not only set yourself free but also create the opportunity for their freedom as well. When that source is no longer feeding your emotions and beliefs, you can see them in a different light. The power they had over you is gone; you have taken back control of your life and your future, and you can now choose to see them through clear lenses. This is not about justifying what they did or accepting it as OK, but it does allow you to see with compassion and understand that they, too, have a journey and a story. They, too, have a source experience that has led them to live a certain way. I've found that when one person finds their freedom, it often leads to the freedom of others. But even if the other person doesn't change, how you interact and how their negative energy and actions impact you will change.

Be sure to give yourself some grace in this process. Simply removing the source does not mean that the behaviors will immediately disappear. In most cases, those behaviors have existed for a long time, and the process of changing them will take time as well. It may seem hard at first, but I can promise you from experience that it gets easier.

Let me briefly review the Framework and tie this together. It begins with us recognizing that we have been settling for a limited life. This limited life has been supported by our behaviors and actions. These behaviors and actions have come from limiting beliefs—lies that we have owned and called truths. These beliefs have come from a source experience. We must identify the limiting beliefs and the sources behind them, and then we can begin the process of healing and resetting our foundation.

Next comes the big question—how? *We cut the cord by replacing the lie of the limiting belief with the truth.* In the faith community, we say these limiting beliefs are ungodly beliefs, contrary to what our Creator says about us and our future. The process involves replacing the ungodly belief with a godly belief. Whether you are a person of faith or not, the process and principle are the same. You must identify the limiting belief and its source, cut the umbilical cord that keeps feeding you, identify the lie, and replace it with the truth. The truth may simply be an opposite declaration—change "I can't" or "I never" to "I can" and "I will." The truth is a positive declaration you begin to make over your life. Don't worry about believing it right away—start declaring it. I promise that as you do, the belief and behaviors will follow.

One of my limiting beliefs came from the experience of abuse by my babysitter. While this source was no longer in my life in any form, the energy was still flowing through that cord. From that experience, I began to look at women differently and believed that all women were manipulative and untrustworthy. I believed that to protect myself, I needed to control those relationships and not allow myself to be taken advantage of. I didn't think I deserved a healthy relationship.

These beliefs caused me to keep women at a distance, avoid intimacy and vulnerability, and eventually hide in pornography and surface-level relationships. This left a wake of broken hearts. As I shared earlier, I did not recognize this until I came to that crossroads in my relationship with my future wife when I had to decide if I was going to run or stay. I was not able to identify why I had been a runner up to that point, but I knew I was done with running and needed to make a pivot and do something different. I replaced the lie of "I am a runner" with a new truth, "I am committed," but my journey to freedom was not over.

The first decade of our marriage was very challenging. My pornography use created distance between me and Melinda, and after ten years, I felt that everything was about to unravel. To make the situation even more intense, we had just adopted our first child, and I was leading a youth ministry in a very large and prominent church in our community. It was through those challenges that I discovered the other limiting beliefs that I was holding on to, as well as the source that was feeding them. This is when I first experienced the process of freedom that I am sharing with you in this book.

The first step of identifying the limiting beliefs and replacing them came from a powerful experience. Up to that point, I thought I had done everything I could to think and act differently. My will was strong, but my freedom was brief. Every time I stumbled, it seemed the pit I was in got deeper. True freedom began with a cry of desperation at three o'clock in the morning.

I'd been driving around our city and pulling into the parking lots of adult venues, sitting in my car wrestling with whether to go in or not. I finally ended up at the church where I worked and sat on the floor in the sanctuary, arguing with God. I don't know your spirituality, and I am not sharing this to convince you to believe what I believe, but this experience has forever changed my life and served as a catalyst for this book.

As I sat there on the sanctuary floor, I began thinking through the beliefs that I held about my life and who I was. It was not pretty. There was a lot of guilt and shame I'd imposed on myself. I remember wondering why I felt this way and believed these things. As I did, the memory of my experience with the babysitter came to mind, as well as other negative experiences. In this moment of desperation, I was led through a process of identifying my limiting (ungodly) beliefs and also their source.

At that moment, I knew what to do. I knew my freedom was tied to forgiveness, not only forgiveness for my source but also for myself. More on that in the next chapter.

I did something else that morning—without this step, my freedom would have been short-lived. Once I had identified all the lies and the source, took responsibility, and sought f orgiveness, my thoughts were filled with the truth about who I was. Every lie that I had declared over myself was being replaced by truth. I wrote each truth down as a declaration on the back of an offering envelope, and I placed that envelope in my wallet, where it remained for at least ten years. It was a constant reminder of the truth about who I was in that area of my life. If I am honest, I did not fully believe the new truths, but I kept declaring them until I did. Anytime I struggled, anytime the lies tried to take root again, I had a response. I had a new belief that I was declaring over myself.

The change in beliefs was immediate, but the change in my behavior was a process. It took time, and as my wife would tell you, I was a work in progress. But it was worth it, and it has led me to where I am today.

Let me be clear—I do not believe your road to freedom must be found through a similar experience. The power of my experience is in the principles and the process I walked through. Those principles and that process are available to anyone at any moment, even right now. That process can release you into the limitless life you were born and created for.

11

The Power of Forgiveness

Forgiveness liberates the soul. It removes fear.
That is why it is such a powerful weapon.
—Nelson Mandela

As I knelt on the floor of my church in the early hours of that pivotal morning, I took a life-changing step. I forgave. I forgave the source of my limiting beliefs—Susan, the babysitter who had abused me so many years ago. I also forgave myself for believing lies. This forgiveness cut the umbilical cord and stopped the flow of negative energy from feeding my limiting beliefs and shaping my mindset. Forgiveness was the knife that set me free.

I'd like to ask your permission to take a brief pause and share a personal belief about forgiveness. As a person of faith, forgiveness is at the very core and is the source of everything I believe. The power of forgiveness is found in a cross and an empty tomb. The power of forgiveness is about love, not law; it is about relationship and identity. I understand that this may not be your belief, and that is OK—it was not mine for a long time. But there is a principle that is true and available to all of us regardless of what we believe. If you think about it, we have all experienced the power of forgiveness in our lives. You do not have to believe as I do to benefit from and experience this freedom and power.

Forgiveness is foundational to experiencing your limitless life. It is a vital part of the process I've been describing throughout this book. Forgiveness is multifaceted. First, there is the forgiveness of self. When you do not forgive yourself even after you have been forgiven, you choose to remain in your prison cell even though the door is unlocked and open. Second, it is about you seeking forgiveness for and taking ownership of the things you have done without excuse or justification. Next, you need to forgive others for the things they have done to you, even if they don't ask for it or deserve it. Forgiveness is about your freedom and releases you to walk in your limitless life. You forgive not because you feel like it but because you know it is the key to your freedom.

While this could be a much deeper conversation, it is important you have an initial and foundational understanding of what forgiveness looks like in each of these areas. The road to your limitless life is not possible without a stop at forgiveness.

Forgive Yourself

When you have identified the lies and limiting beliefs you have held over your life, the first step is to forgive yourself for believing them. For a person of faith, it might sound something like this: "God, forgive me for believing the lie that I am not good enough. Forgive me for believing the lie that I am not smart enough." Here's what I said: "Forgive me for believing the lie that all women desire to use and hurt me. Forgive me for believing I am worthless when you call me worthy." If faith is not your source of freedom, you may also turn this around and make the statement, "I forgive myself for and release myself from the lie . . . and choose to believe the truth that I am. . . ." This may feel and sound awkward, but I encourage you to trust the process. You are releasing yourself from the power of those limiting beliefs; you're going a level deeper than when you flushed the paper down the toilet. Understand that with forgiveness comes a desire and a choice to change your thoughts, beliefs, and behaviors. When you forgive yourself for believing a lie, you need to replace it with the truth, as in my example above. I replaced worthless with worthy.

Asking for Forgiveness

Think of a time in your life when you realized your actions had caused pain for someone else. Maybe it was something you said out of anger or fear. Maybe it was something you did or didn't do. We've all had those moments where we've done something or said something and immediately wished we could take it back, but we knew it was too late and the damage had been done. You had a choice at that moment— move on and pretend it never happened, or go to the person you hurt and apologize, acknowledging what you did and asking them to forgive you.

If you went to them and apologized and owned your actions, even if they did not receive it, you experienced the power and release that is found in forgiveness. Forgiveness, at its core, is not first about the other person (and it's not about letting them off the hook), it's about you and your freedom. Asking for forgiveness can be one of the most difficult things we ever do, but I know from my experience and the testimony of others that the forgiven heart experiences freedom, joy, and restoration. Forgiveness is powerful. It's like removing a heavy weight. At that moment, it's as though you have received a fresh start and a clean slate. By taking ownership of your role, you become free of the guilt and shame associated with wronging another.

From a faith perspective, it is important to understand that God never justifies sin (or negative behavior), even as a response to someone else's sin. It's like the old saying—two wrongs don't make a right. Don't get caught up in the blame game, trying to justify your sins by pointing to someone else's.

An example would be the disrespectful way I treated women in my early years. Those actions can never be justified by the experience I had with my babysitter. Both were wrong, and both require forgiveness. When I am asking for forgiveness, I am taking responsibility for my actions. Although I cannot control the things that are done to me or around me, I am always able to control my response to those things.

Here is another hard truth—if you ask for forgiveness in hopes that it will change someone's behavior, it is not really forgiveness you are asking for. That is more like manipulation. When you seek forgiveness, the goal is not to elicit a certain response. This is about your freedom and your future.

What if the other person doesn't grant forgiveness? Asking for forgiveness is about the posture of your heart and your desire to do the right thing and take responsibility for your actions. Your freedom does not rely on someone's acceptance of your request for forgiveness but on your sincere heart that seeks forgiveness. Remember—this process is about the things we can control, not the things we can't. This is about your freedom and the limitless life that is waiting for you.

Forgiving Others

When you have identified a person as the source of a limiting belief, it's time to forgive them and release them to their own journey. This can feel hard, but remember—it's about you. This is where you put the knife to the umbilical cord and stop the flow of negative energy. This is your declaration that you will no longer allow someone else's actions and choices to control your freedom and your future. Maybe the hardest thing to understand about forgiving others is that it is a choice and not a feeling.

Saying "I forgive you" is not about accepting or ignoring sinful actions. It is not about saving someone from the natural consequences associated with their actions. Forgiveness does not equal a restored relationship (reconciliation cannot happen without forgiveness, but forgiveness does not equal reconciliation).

Forgiving someone is ultimately about your freedom; you refuse to be bound to someone else's actions. When you choose not to forgive and hold on to resentment or bitterness, you are binding yourself to that person. When you offer forgiveness, you set yourself free from the umbilical attachment created by the negative action.

You can forgive someone without them asking you for forgiveness or even admitting they have done something wrong. You must believe that the road to your freedom is not tied to their repentance but to your release of them. Aren't you tired of allowing someone else's actions and brokenness to control your emotions and keep you from the limitless life you were born and created for?

This is how forgiveness worked in my story. I was able to cut the umbilical cord from Susan that had been feeding me lies for all those years, even though she did not ask for forgiveness, and I haven't seen her since I was a child. Here is what I declared:

- Susan, I forgive you for taking physical advantage of me as a child and for stealing my innocence. I will no longer allow you and that experience to shape my beliefs about my identity.

- Susan, I forgive you for leading me to believe that I was responsible for the actions you took against me. I will no longer allow those beliefs to shape how I value women and myself.

After saying those words, I walked through the process of forgiving myself for believing the lies that had shown up in my life as a result of my experience, and I replaced the lies with the truth.

- God forgive me for (*or* I forgive myself for) believing that what happened to me was my fault. I choose to believe that I did nothing wrong and that I am good.
- God forgive me for (*or* I forgive myself for) believing that all women want to use me and hurt me. I choose to believe that women are created in the image of God and are valuable and make me better.

When you make these statements, they may feel like empty words, but there is a spiritual transaction that is taking place in your life. Words are powerful, your declarations mean something, and they are the first step to rewiring your subconscious mind and moving away from the lies you have believed and the behaviors you have be*lived*.

The road to the limitless life runs through forgiveness.

12

Putting It All Together

*Continuous effort—not strength or intelligence—
is the key to unlocking and using our potential.*
—Liane Cordes

A s I write this book, my hope and prayer is that you will catch a vision for your life that is greater than you could have ever thought, hoped, or imagined. I've shared my story and the principles and processes I have learned over the last thirty years so that you, too, can see the power of your story and the potential of its unwritten pages. Along the way, you have learned how to crush limiting beliefs, cultivate an infinite mindset, and unleash your true potential. In this chapter, I will summarize the process of releasing your limitless life so that you can make this journey your own.

As I'm sure you have discovered along the way, walking into a limitless life demands courage and a willingness to face yourself and the hard truth about your trauma and behavior. It involves discomfort and stretching. It challenges what you believe and the source of your beliefs, perhaps even bringing you to let go of some relationships along the way.

It's important to understand that you are in control of what this looks like for you. While I believe the principles I've shared are non-negotiable truths, each reader's journey is personal. This is not a linear process; it is fluid and will flow in different directions as you dig deeper into the beliefs that are driving your behaviors as well as the sources and experiences that shaped those beliefs. You may enter the process at any point, moving back and forth until you have completely cut the umbilical cord tying you to the specific source or experience feeding your limiting belief.

Stepping into your limitless life begins with a personal revelation—the belief that your current reality does not have to define your future possibilities. You are only limited by what you believe and the narrative you choose to tell yourself about your experiences. While your experiences are real and their impact is powerful, they do not have the final say in who you are and what is possible in your life.

Once you have embraced the truth that you were born limitless and have recognized that you are settling for and living in a less-than life, you are ready to enter the process that leads to transformation and freedom.

The process that led you to your limited life is the same process that you can use to get to your limitless life. The difference is the source of your beliefs and how you interpret or define your experiences. This is where you get to choose and declare a new thought and give yourself a new foundation to build new beliefs and create new behaviors.

The Born Limitless Framework

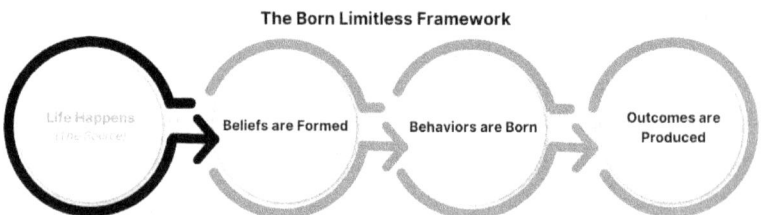

Life Happens (the Source) → Beliefs are Formed → Behaviors are Born → Outcomes are Produced

My life (and the lives of many others) is proof that this sequence can be disrupted—no matter what happened in your past, you, too, can change your future. But different outcomes require different behaviors, different behaviors require different decisions, different decisions require different beliefs, and different beliefs require different thoughts. If your behaviors and outcomes are ever going to change, you will have to address your beliefs as well as the sources and experiences that created those beliefs.

Where you start addressing these issues is where the personalization comes in. Here are some examples of "points of entry" along the process.

- You look at the outcomes you are producing and realize that you have been settling for a less-than life, and it's time to make a change.

- You realize the way you have been doing things is not producing the results you desire. You recognize that your behaviors often lead to disagreements, failed outcomes, and strained relationships.

- You start asking yourself why you do what you do, and you don't like the answers. You begin noticing that your beliefs are leading to behaviors that you are not proud of.

- You notice that every time you are around a certain person or when they are brought up in conversation, your energy and attitude change. You find yourself becoming impatient and argumentative.

- You know that your attitudes and behaviors in certain situations are not OK, but you cannot figure out where the attitudes and behaviors come from.

What's next? This is where you start to ask yourself difficult questions and get honest with the answers.

1. Identify your limiting beliefs one at a time. See the lists you made in Chapters Five and Six for reference.

2. Acknowledge each limiting belief as a lie and choose to pivot away from that belief.

3. Repent and forgive yourself for believing those lies and allowing them to impact your behaviors.

4. Recognize and identify the source—a person or experience—that has led to your beliefs and impacted your behaviors and actions.

5. Forgive and release any person who is a source of limiting beliefs. When you do this, you are cutting the umbilical cord between you and the source feeding you the lie.

6. Choose to no longer allow the source to inform your beliefs and drive your behaviors.

7. Replace each limiting belief with truth and begin to declare that truth over your life.

It's important to understand that changing behavior takes time. You did not end up where you are overnight. Your freedom begins when you adopt a new, more positive, and powerful belief and then start declaring that belief and walking it out daily. I often suggest that people share their new beliefs and desired behaviors with trusted friends and family members who can help remind and encourage them along the way. This is where giving yourself some grace becomes important.

Now is a chance for you to put this process into practice. Choose a limiting belief that is easily recognizable and one you have been dealing with for some time. Do you have one? Now, walk that limiting belief through the process.

1. Identify and denounce the limiting belief/lie (this is typically an "I can't," "I won't," "I'm not," or "I never" statement): _____

   _____

   _____

   _____

2. Forgive yourself. "I choose to forgive myself for believing (name the limiting belief or lie) _____
   _____ and allowing it to (write how it is impacting your life and relationships negatively)
   _____.
   I choose to believe the truth that _____
   _____.

3. Identify the source (person/people or experience):
   _____.

4. Choose to forgive the source. If a person: "I forgive
   _____ and will no longer allow him/her/them to shape my beliefs about myself or what I am capable of. I release them to their own process." If the source is not tied to a person but rather an experience: "I choose to release this experience and no longer allow (name the experience as able) _____
   ___ _____ to shape my beliefs and influence my behaviors. I am free!"

5. Write and declare out loud the new truth as a positive declaration over your life (this can be in the form of an "I am," "I can," or "I will" statement): _____
   _____
   _____.
   (This is what you will return to as you begin to change your behaviors).

That is the guide. I encourage you to make it your own. Crushing and replacing your limiting beliefs is the first step in the transformation process of creating new behaviors that lead to new outcomes. Anchoring the new belief will be critical in sustaining the behavioral change necessary to truly walk out the limitless life you were born and created for. The anchoring process begins with repeated declarations, written reminders, and connecting your new beliefs with new behaviors.

The process that I have shared with you is powerful and foundational. True transformation is not experienced through intellect alone. To experience sustained transformation in our lives, we must choose to believe it is possible and that we are capable. We must be committed to declaring life and truth over ourselves daily until it becomes our new "normal."

You must move forward with a clear vision and a belief that there is something more, something greater, that you were created and born for. That is ultimately the catalyst that will keep you moving when the process gets hard. Without a clear vision and destination, the challenges will stop you in your tracks, and you'll retreat to those comfort zones. Get a clear destination in mind—know your vision. Having a map is a vital process in reaching your destination with limited detours—that is the focus of my short and practical book, *The Roadmap to Significance.*

I opened this book with the following assertion: *Born Limitless* is ultimately about my belief that every one of us was born with potential and the ability to live a life of significance. We started the journey by defining a limitless life and the mindset we must adopt that says we can do anything we put our minds to. This is your birthright and something you need to contend for. Your legacy, influence, and impact are at stake. When you first declared that you were born limitless, you might not have believed it. My prayer as we near the close of this book is that you can now make this declaration from a place of belief and that you can see a way through.

Remember the light at the end of the tunnel I mentioned in the first chapter? I promise you it is not an oncoming train.

Anytime doubt creeps in, fear pokes its head out, or there's a temptation to quit and return to something familiar, declare these words over your life, get up, and go get that limitless life you were born and created for:

I am created for more—more influence and impact, more future and more hope.

I believe that I was born limitless and that I will experience and walk in my limitless life.

Where Do We Go from Here?

D o you remember the GPS I mentioned in Section Two? Every GPS needs two locations to create a map, and so far, you've established the first—where you are now. Now, you need a clear picture of your destination.

We all need a compelling vision of our future. Without it, we will wander aimlessly. I don't know what your limitless life looks like or what the *more* is that you were born and created for, but I do know that you have now set the foundation to dream again. It's time to live beyond the moment you are standing in and ask, "What is truly possible? What am I capable of? What am I passionate about? What legacy do I desire to leave behind?"

Your next step is to move from accidental to intentional living around a clear vision. You can then begin to build the roadmap necessary to reach every destination you set your mind and heart to.

- A dream written down with a date becomes a goal.
- A goal broken down into steps becomes a plan.
- A plan backed by action makes your dreams a reality.

If you're ready to become strategic and intentional and build that roadmap, I would love to help you in the process. I invite you to check out my other book, *The Roadmap to Significance*. That is where I share how you can create a life that is more than successful—it is significant.

Success is all about me and dies when I die.

Significance is about purpose, something bigger than me, and that lasts well beyond my lifetime.

If you have experienced freedom, have begun to dream again, and are ready to fully embrace your true potential, then it's time to make the leap from success to significance.

The Roadmap to Significance is an MBA on significance in one book, an in-depth look at what you were created for. You will be challenged to widen your definition and lens of success so that you can live a life of true value. You will learn strategies and identifiers to help you make the choices necessary to have long-term sustainable success and endurance. Achieve greater success for a longer time by becoming part of the eight percent of people who reach their goals.

Thank you for taking this journey with me. I pray it has been impactful and transformational for you. I conclude all my podcasts and messages with the same statement, and I would like to share that with you here:

My name is Rick Torrison, and I'm believing your best is yet to come. I believe you were created for more. Not more stuff—but more influence and impact, more future and hope. I don't know what your more is, but my passion is to help you discover it and to walk it out.

God bless you!

Endnotes

1   This is a quotation from A Knight's Tale (John Thatcher as he says goodbye to his young son), screenplay by Brian Helgeland.

2   Allen, James. As a Man Thinketh. United Kingdom: Sheldon University Press, 1908.

3   Ibid.

4   The Everyday Life Bible The Power of God's Word for Everyday Living, 9781478922971.

5   Vital, Anna. "The Number of Failures before Success [Infographic]." Personal Excellence, July 2, 2022. https://personalexcellence.co/blog/failure-infographic/.

6   This is a quotation from Finding Nemo, screenplay by Andrew Stanton, Bob Peterson, and David Reynolds.

7   Thompson, Karl. "What Is Normal?" ReviseSociology, August 31, 2018. https://revisesociology.com/2018/09/03/what-is-normal/.

8   Vaish, A., Grossmann, T., & Woodward, A. (2008). "Not all emotions are created equal: the negativity bias in social-emotional development." Psychological Bulletin, 134(3), 383–403.

9   Carretié, L., Mercado, F., Tapia, M., & Hinojosa, J. A. (2001). "Emotion, attention, and the 'negativity bias,' studied through event-related potentials." International Journal of Psychophysiology, 41(1), 75–85.

10 "Our Brain's Negative Bias." Psychology Today. Sussex Publishers. Accessed March 8, 2023. https://www.psychologytoday.com/us/articles/200306/our-brains-negative-bias.

Born Limitless Framework

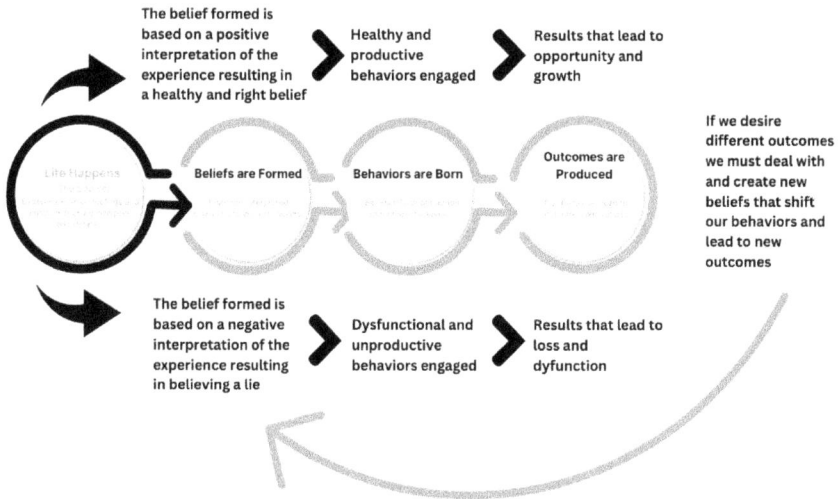

The belief formed is based on a positive interpretation of the experience resulting in a healthy and right belief

Healthy and productive behaviors engaged

Results that lead to opportunity and growth

If we desire different outcomes we must deal with and create new beliefs that shift our behaviors and lead to new outcomes

Life Happens

Beliefs are Formed

Behaviors are Born

Outcomes are Produced

The belief formed is based on a negative interpretation of the experience resulting in believing a lie

Dysfunctional and unproductive behaviors engaged

Results that lead to loss and dyfunction

Acknowledgments

Deep gratitude and thanks to my writing coach, Daphne, who helped me believe in myself and the value of my message. Her encouragement and direction kept me moving forward.

To my editor, Abigail, who has the patience of Job. Thank you for asking the hard questions and helping me translate what was in my heart onto the pages.

A special thank you to my incredible clients who have trusted me through their journey. I'm grateful they allowed me to serve them and add to their growth.

About the Author

Rick Torrison is the visionary founder of Right Now Leadership LLC and Revival Rivers Non-Profit, with an established international presence as an author, sought-after speaker, and certified Success & John C. Maxwell coach. With more than aquarter-century of hands-on experience, Rick has emerged as a widely respected authority specializinginhelpingpassionate and growth-minded leaders unlock the full potential of their identity.

Rick has collaborated with an array of Fortune 500 corporations, including HCA Healthcare and State Farm. His expertise lies in strengthening teams and coaching leaders to achieve their highest potential. Rick is most passionate about serving entrepreneurs, solopreneurs, and leaders at every level. With a Doctorate in Community Transformation and specialized certifications in DISC, communication, accountability, and coaching, he's a trusted authority in the field.

Rick's thought leadership has been showcased in various professional publications, notably American CEO and Somebody Cares International magazines, amplifying his influence in the realms of leadership, communication, and personal growth.

Pioneering a proprietary coaching process, Rick employs a set of six powerful questions to guide individuals and organizations in constructing their Roadmap to Significance. This transformative approach systematically dismantles limiting beliefs, paving the way for the realization and utilization of one's true identity.

Whether you're an individual wrestling with self-imposed constraints or an organization seeking to elevate its collective productivity, Rick Torrison provides the strategic insights and tactical expertise required for impactful growth and enduring success.

Elevate your leadership journey with Rick Torrison, and step into the full power of your identity today.

Connect with Rick at RickTorrison.com

FOLLOW AND CONNECT WITH AUTHOR, SPEAKER, AND COACH
RICK TORRISON

Discover your true purpose and unlock your full potential personally and professionally.

Visit RickTorrison.com and access free tips, assessments, videos, and personal coaching opportunities with Rick.

Follow Rick on ALL social media platforms.

Scan the QR code to join The Limitless Leader private Facebook community to stay connected, be encouraged, and receive priority access to all programs and free resources and tools exclusively for community members.

RickTorrison.com

Download Your Limitless Leader Toolkit and Other FREE Resources Today.

Become The Limitless Leader You Were Born and Created For

Your personal toolkit includes:

- **Personal growth and leadership Assessment.**
  You will never get where you are going without first understanding where you are starting from.

- **Access to The Limitless Leader private community.**
  Surround yourself with like-minded, growth-minded individuals committed to adding value to each other.

- **An electronic copy of As a Man Thinketh by James Allen.**
  A classic take on the power of your thoughts and beliefs on your behaviors and outcomes.

- **The Limitless Leader 5-day challenge.**
  A fully automated foundation-setting journey to help identify, crush, and replace limiting beliefs.

and more...

Believing Your Best is Yet to Come!

Resources.BornLimitlessBook.com

Printed in the USA
CPSIA information can be obtained
at www.ICGtesting.com
LVHW020415150524
780334LV00016B/826

9 781636 802022